EDITION EUROS

BRUNO GMÜNDER ■

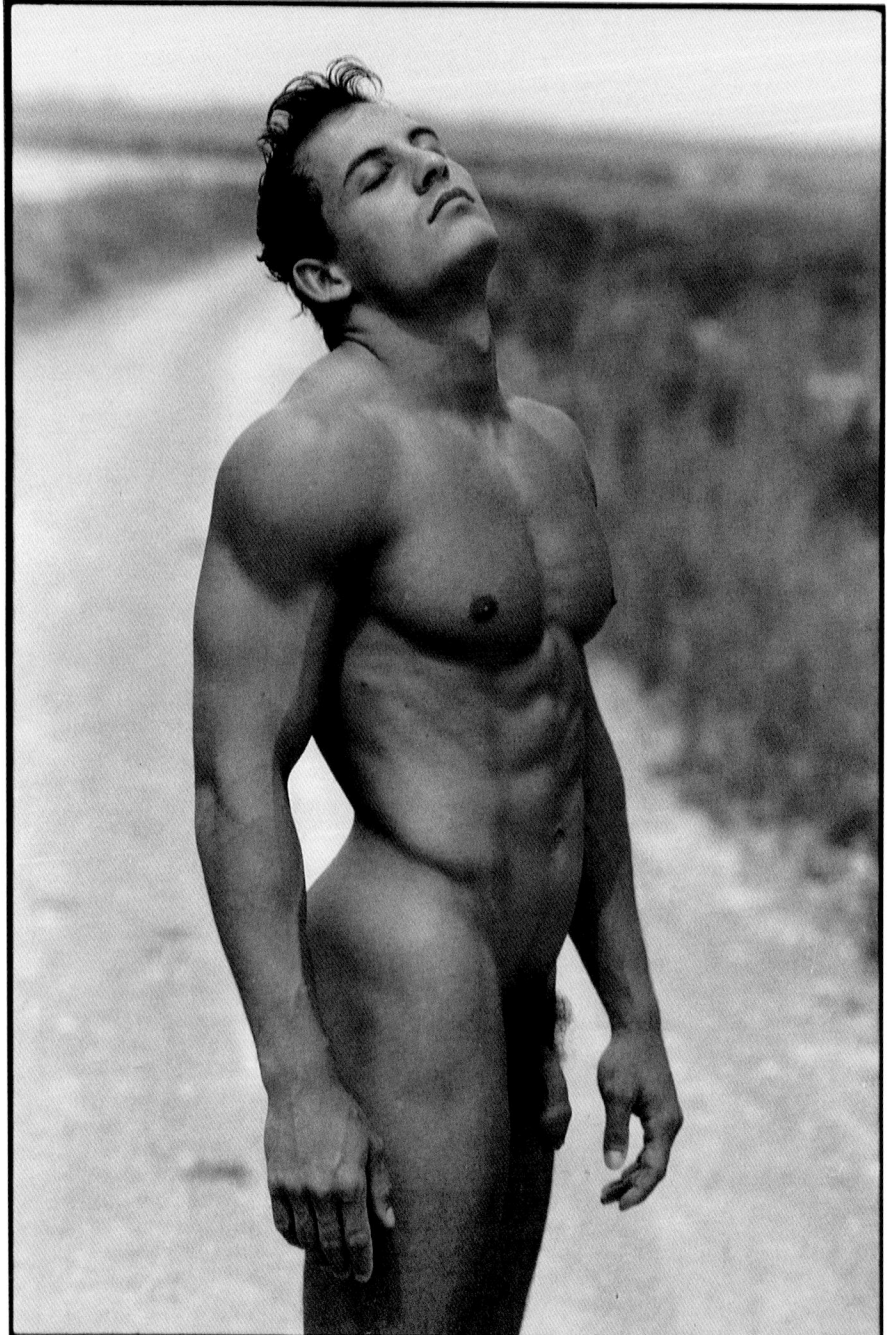

EDITION EUROS 5

JOSÉ MESSANA

BRUNO GMÜNDER

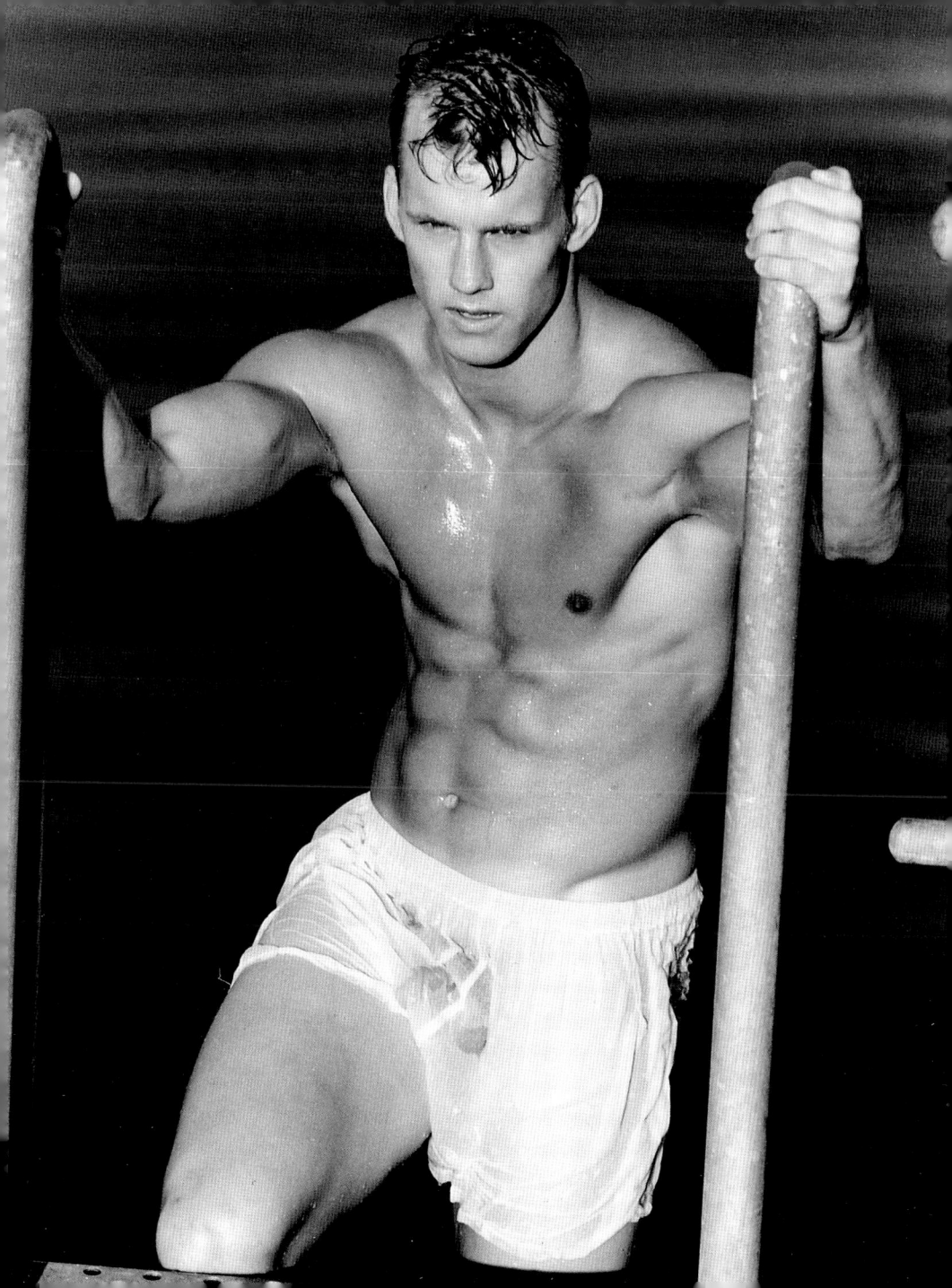

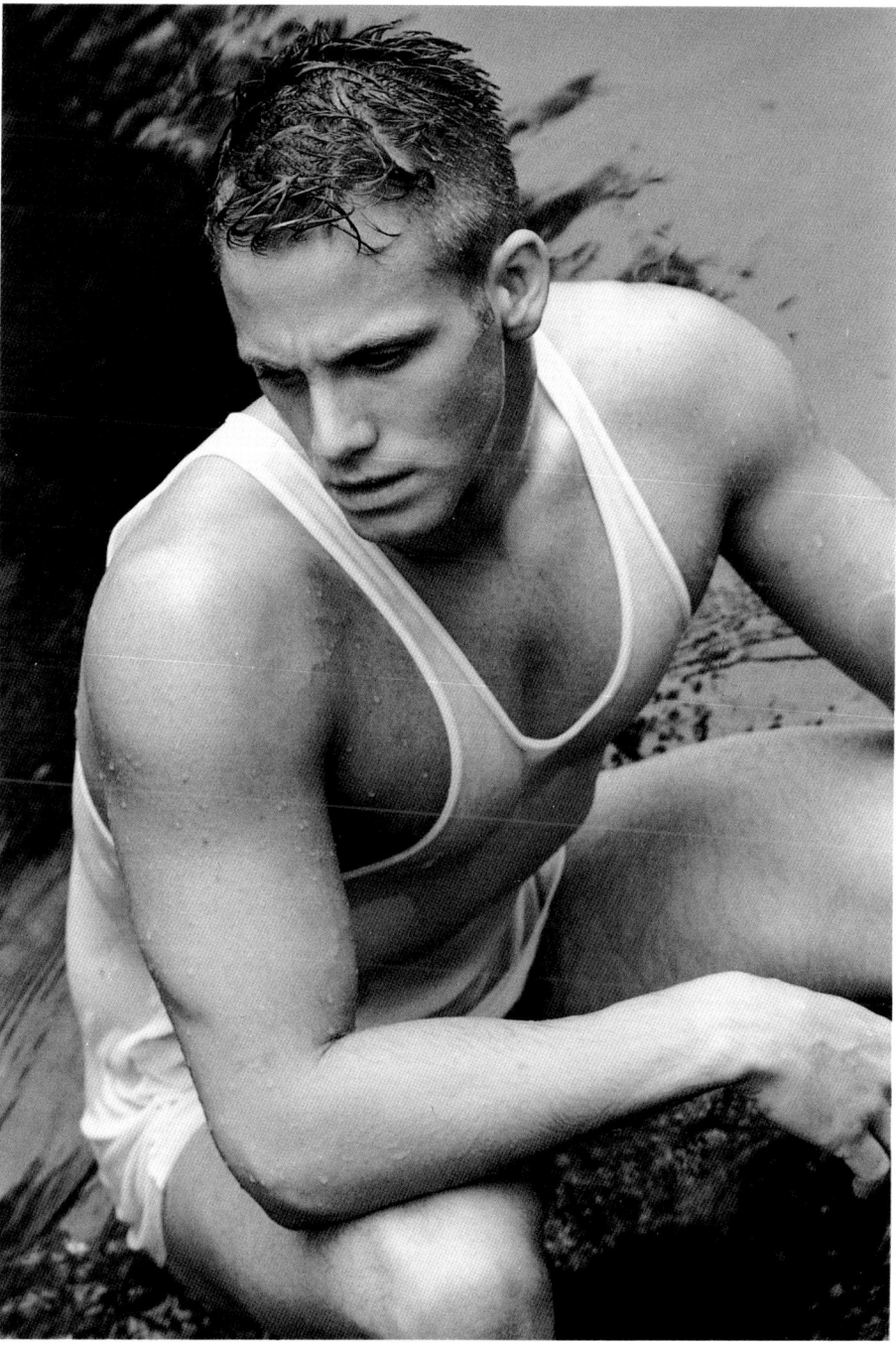

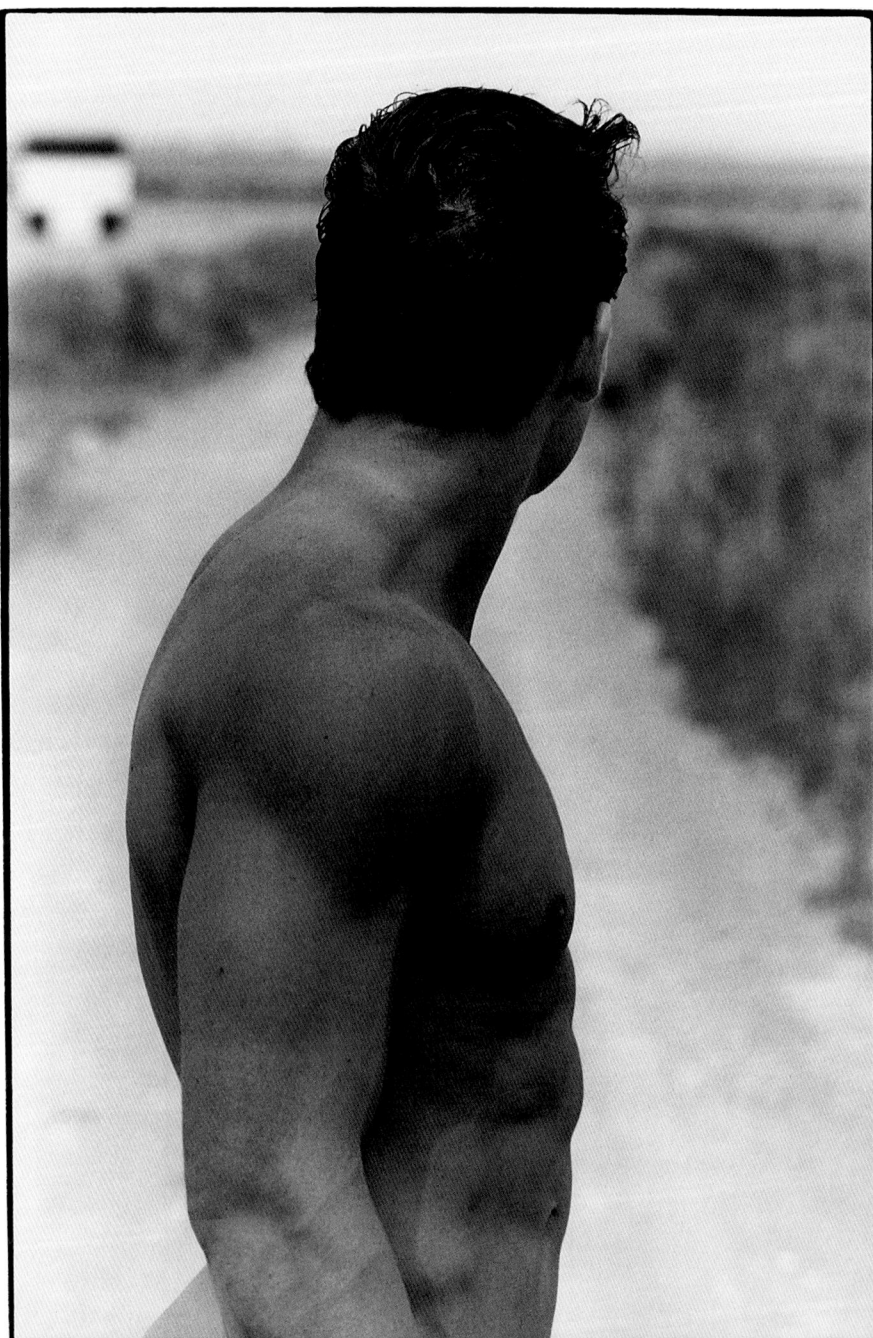

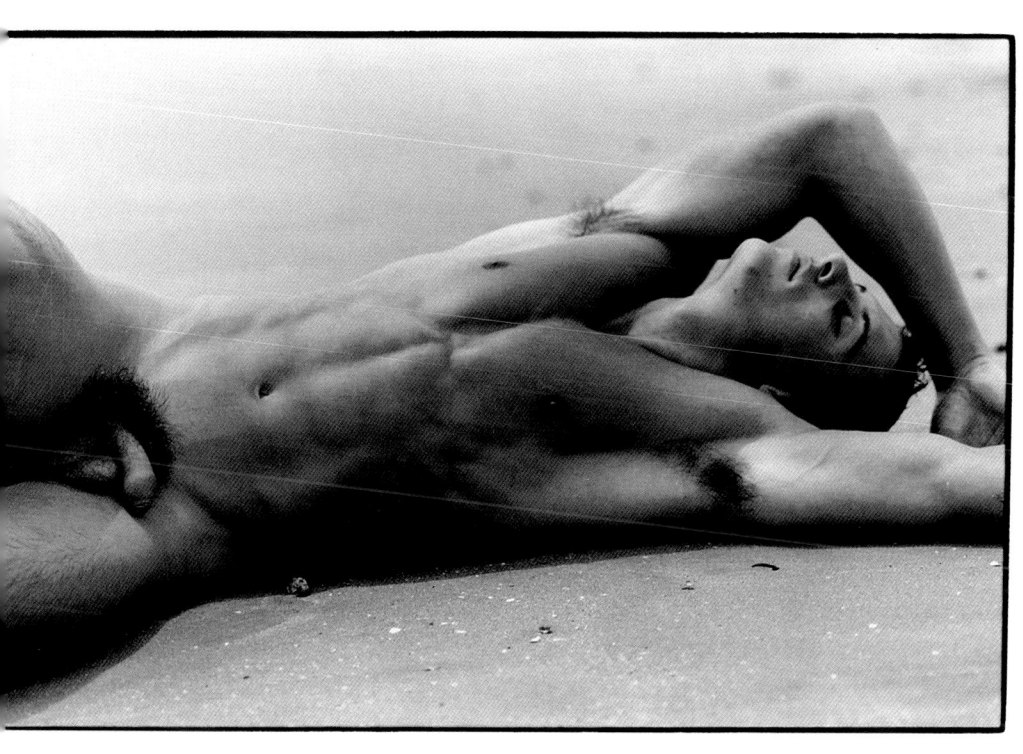

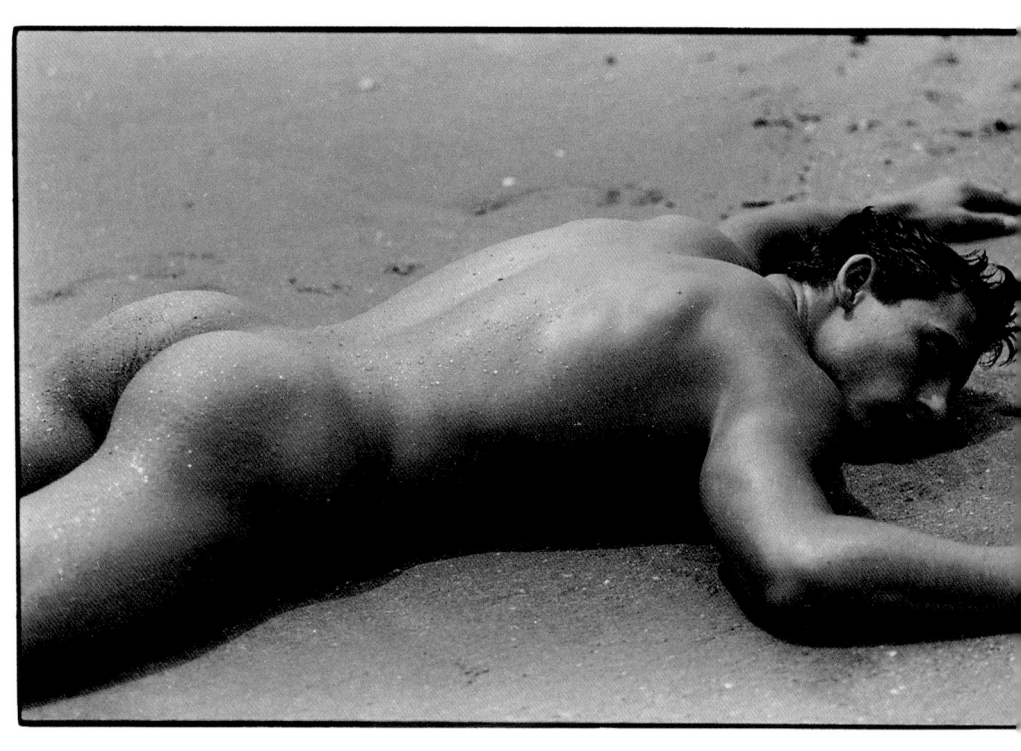

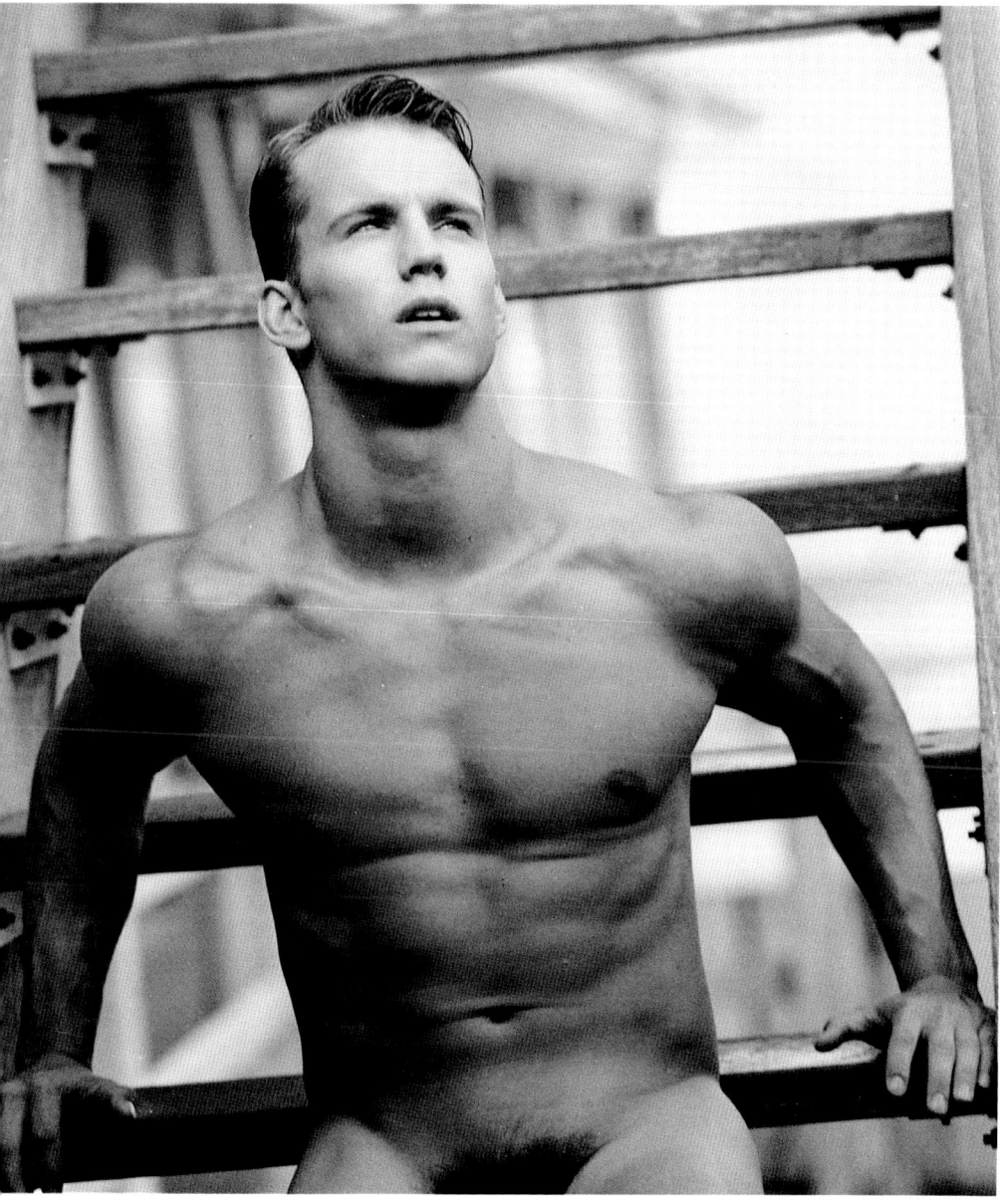

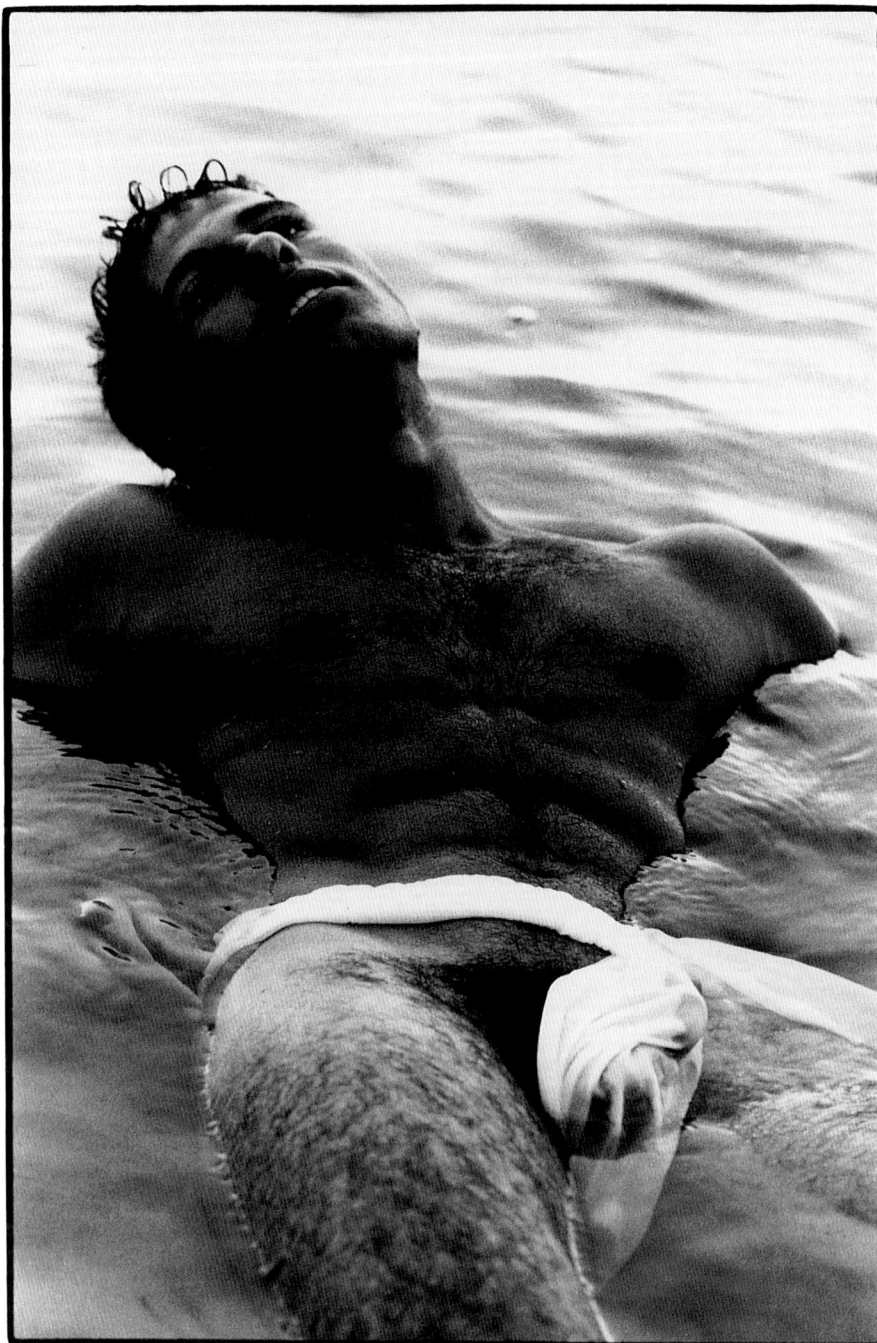

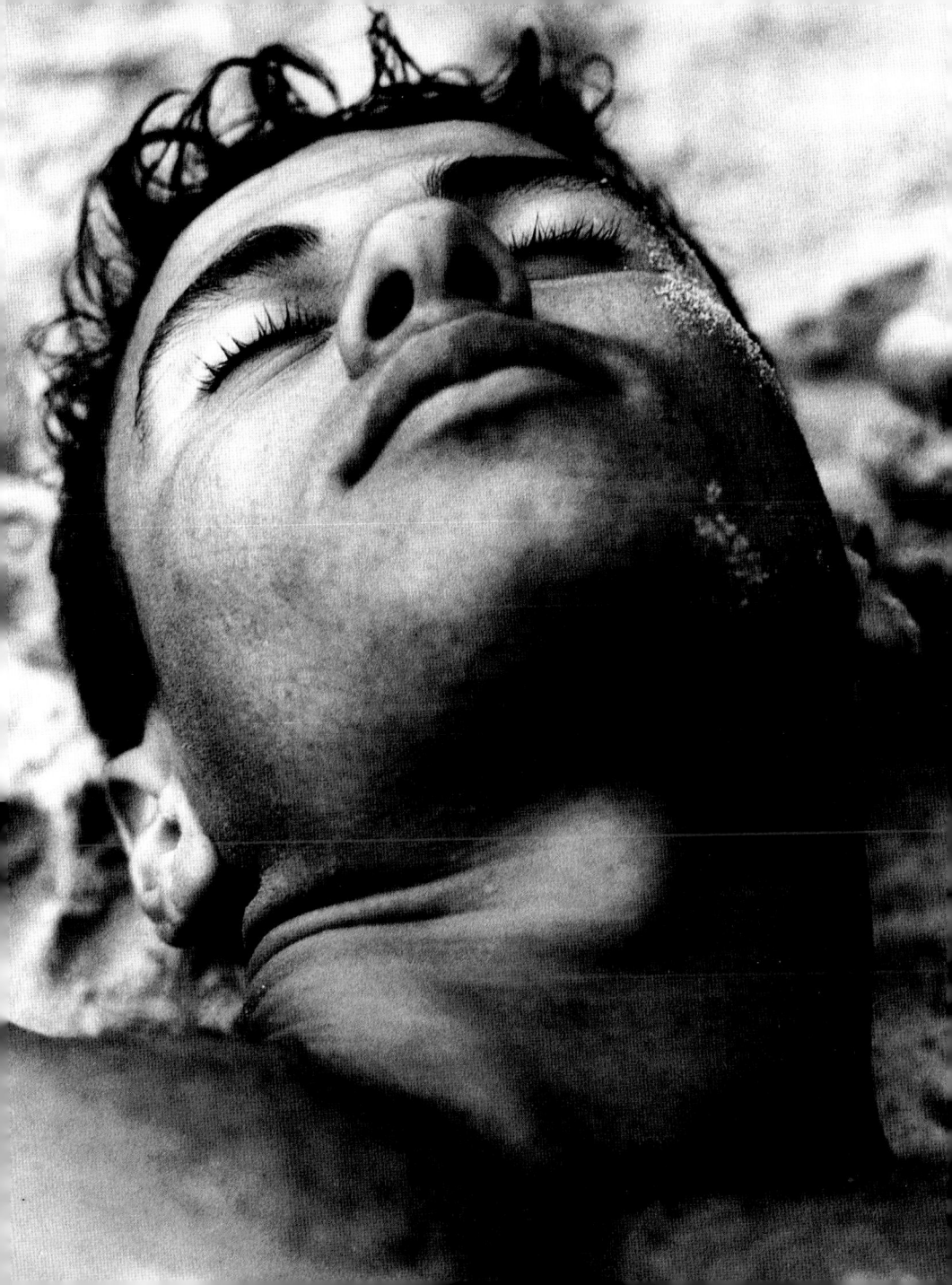

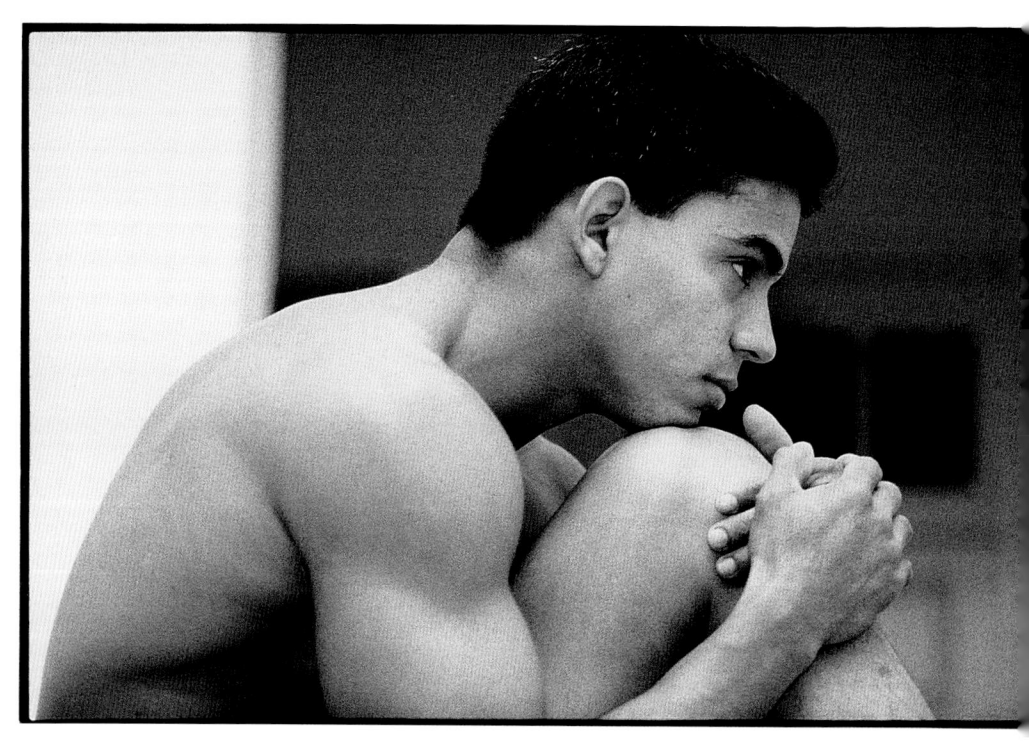

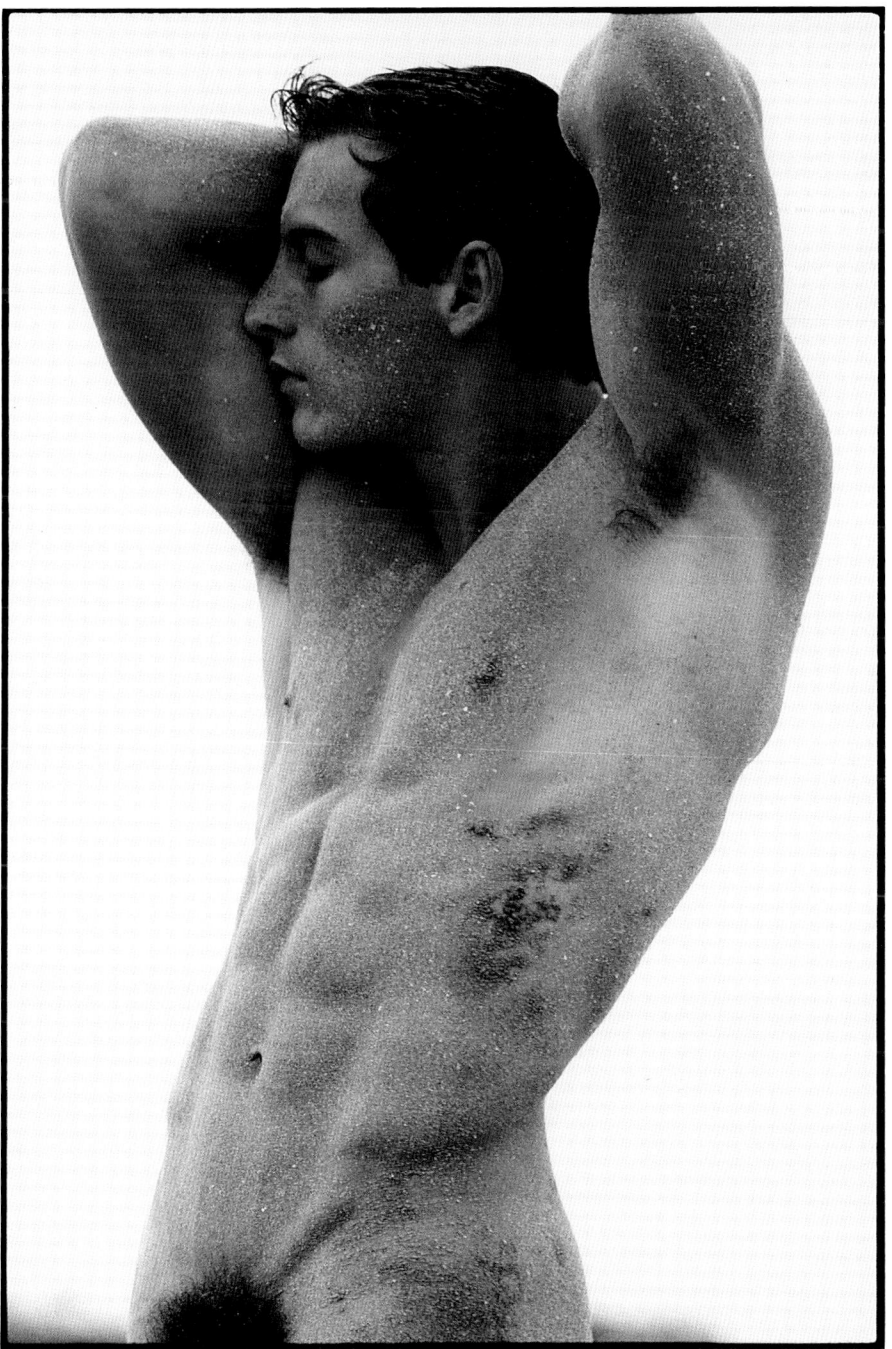

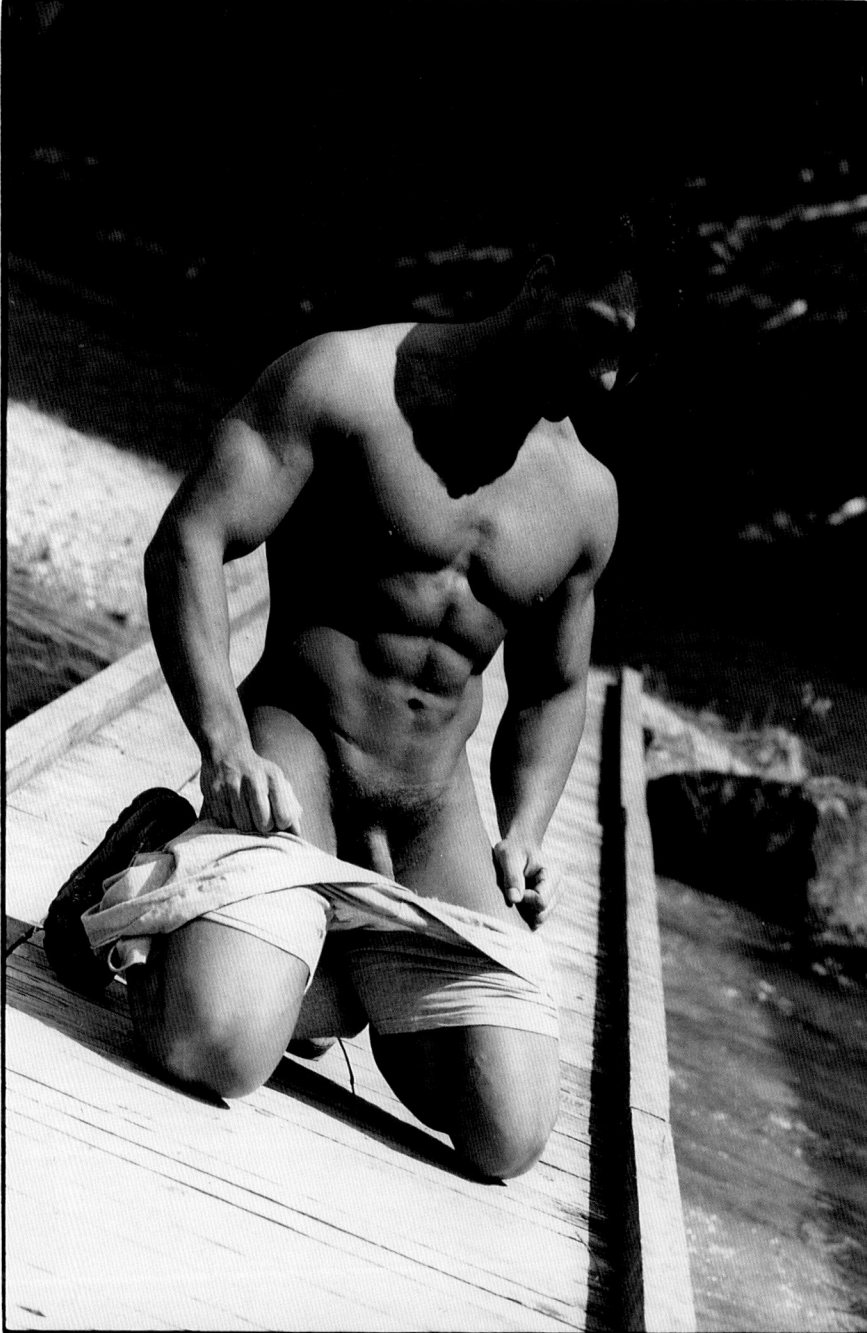

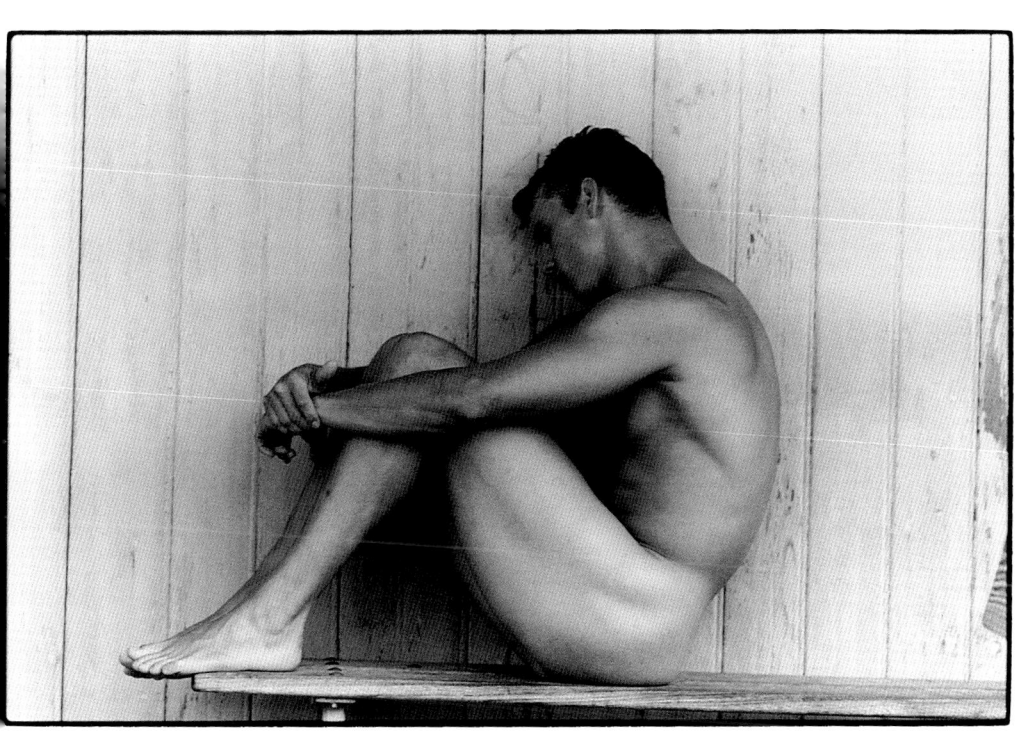

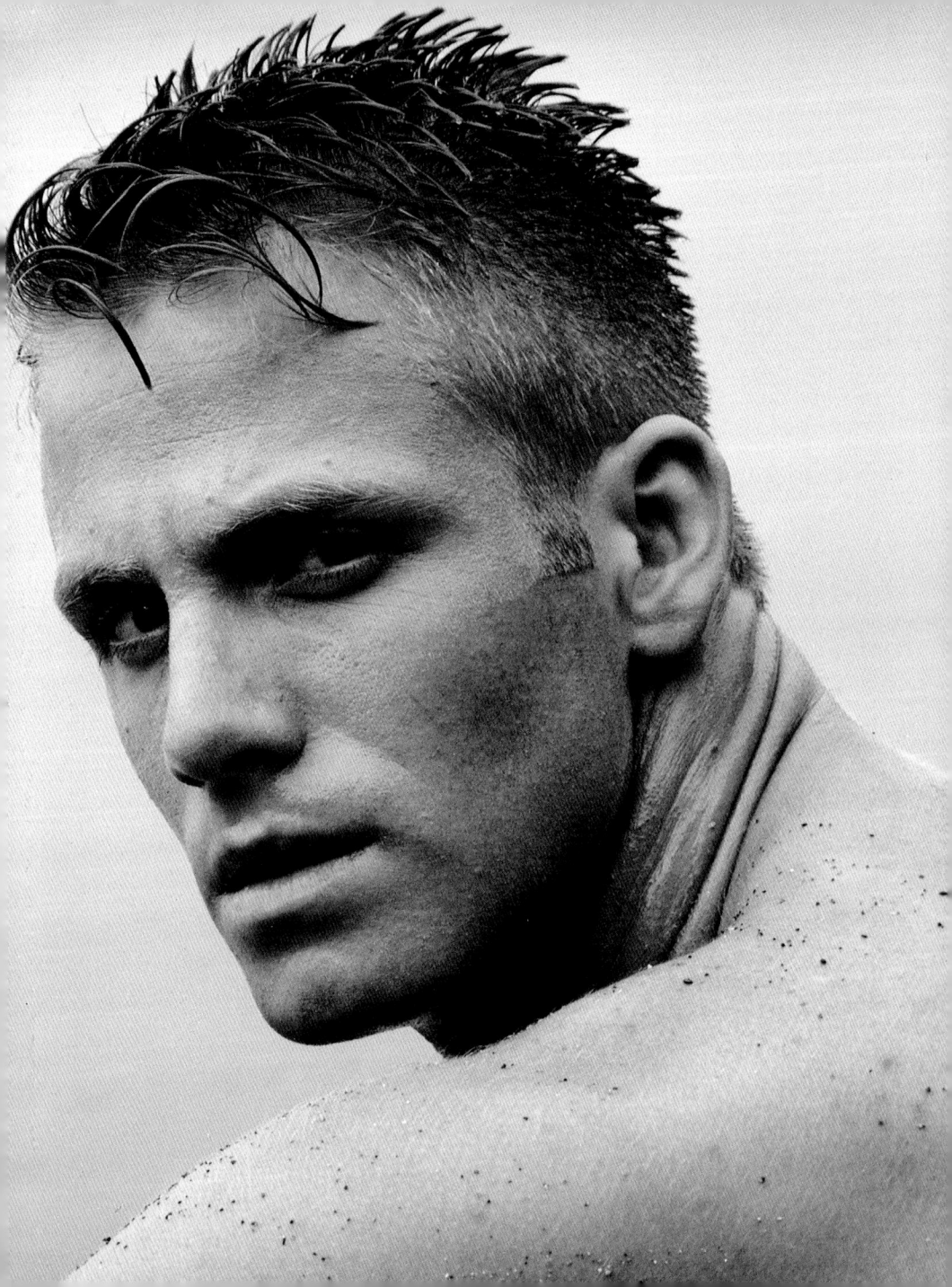

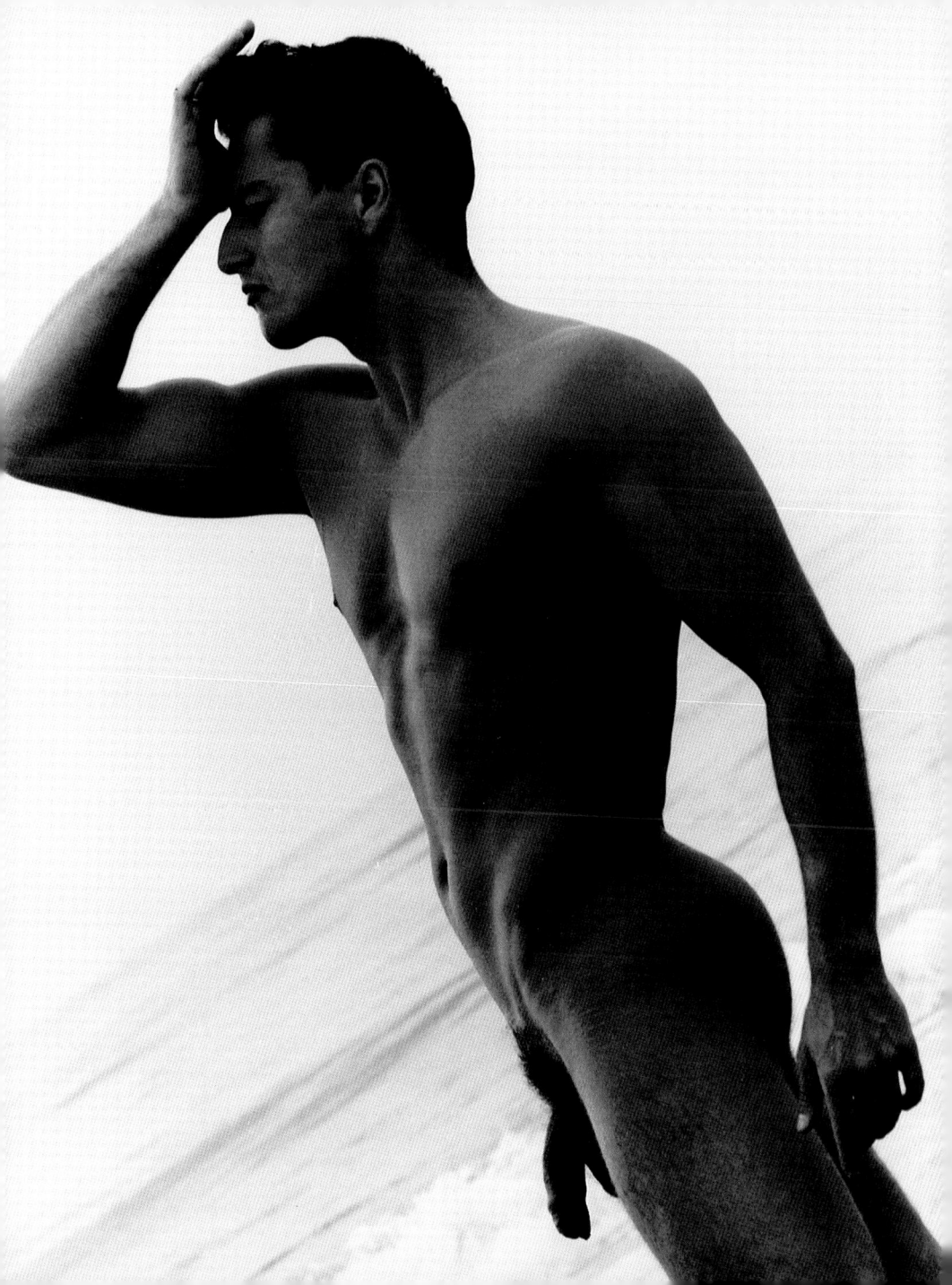

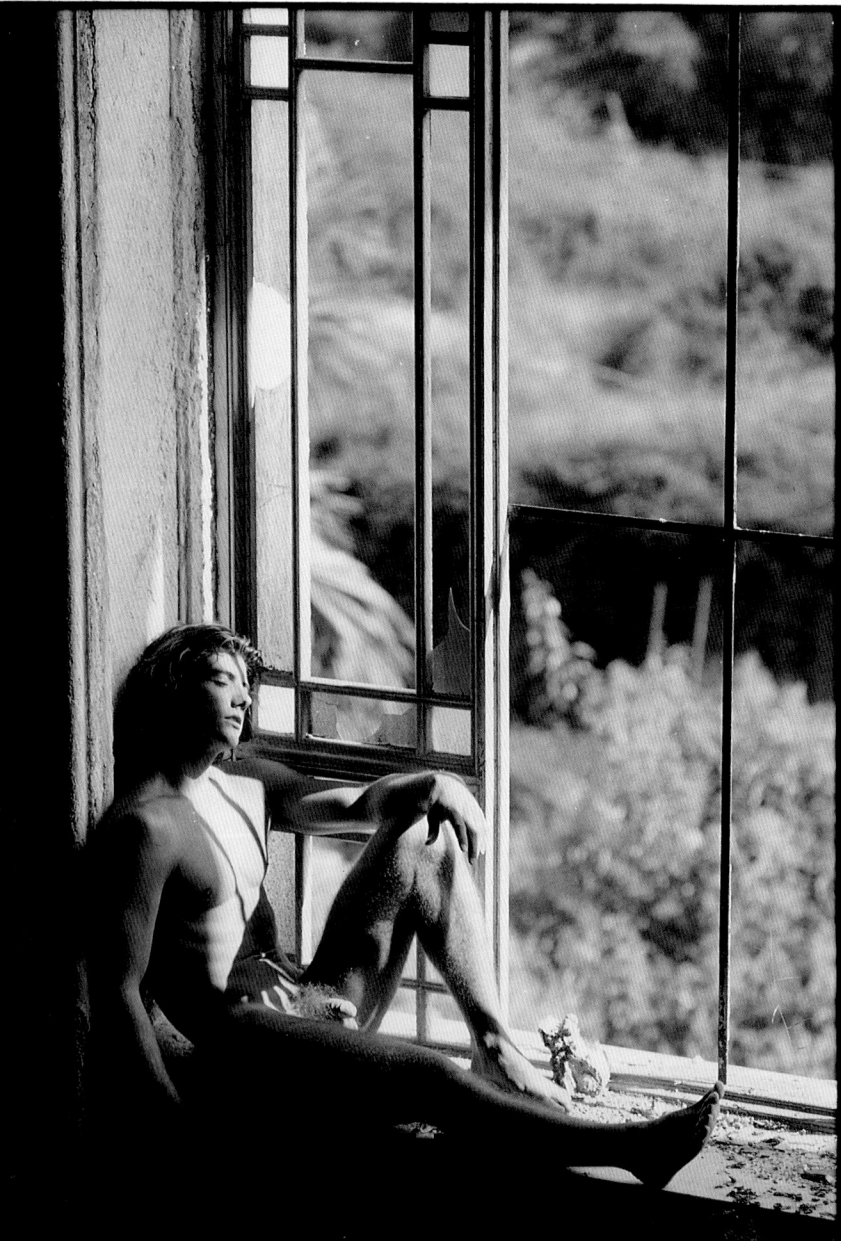

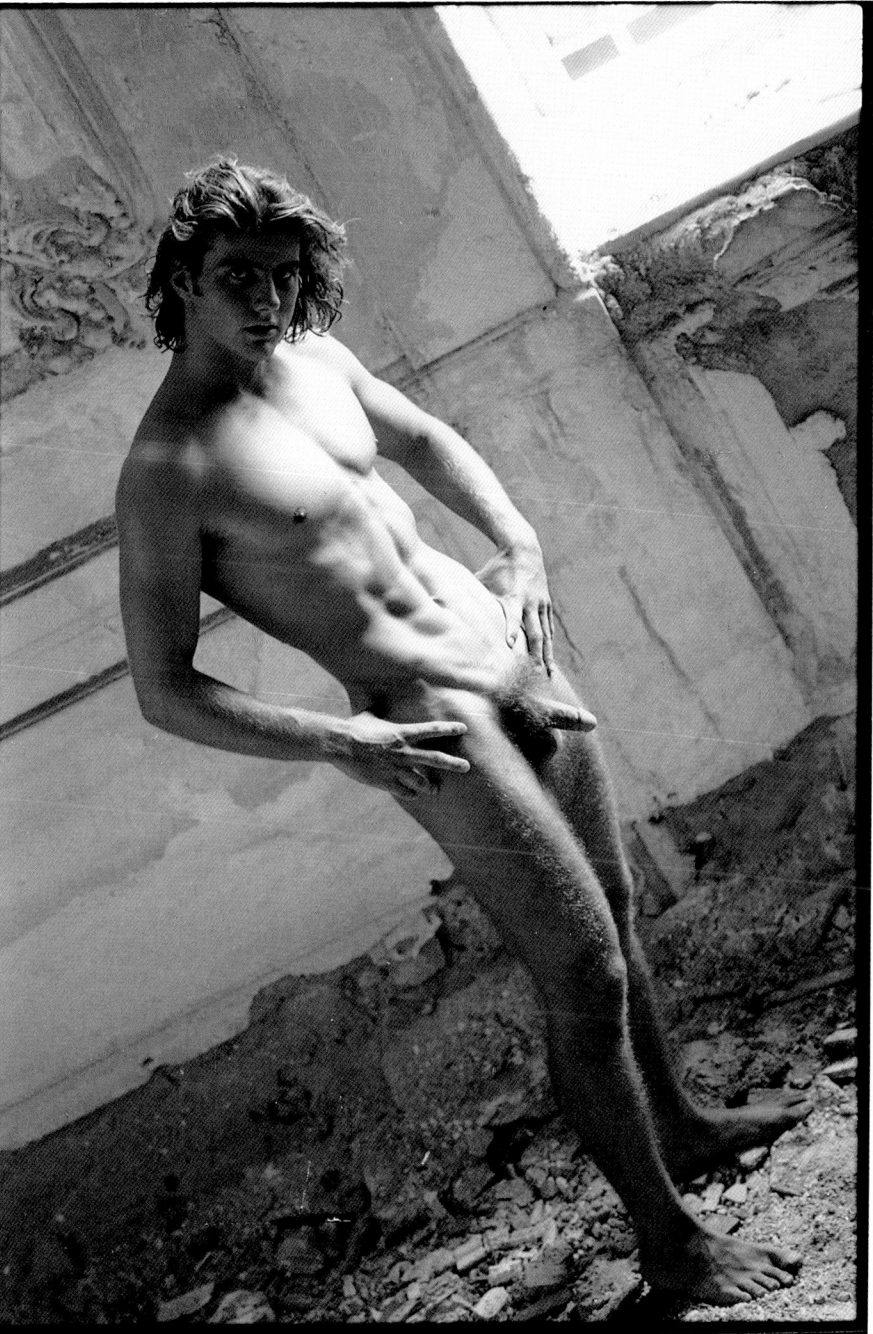

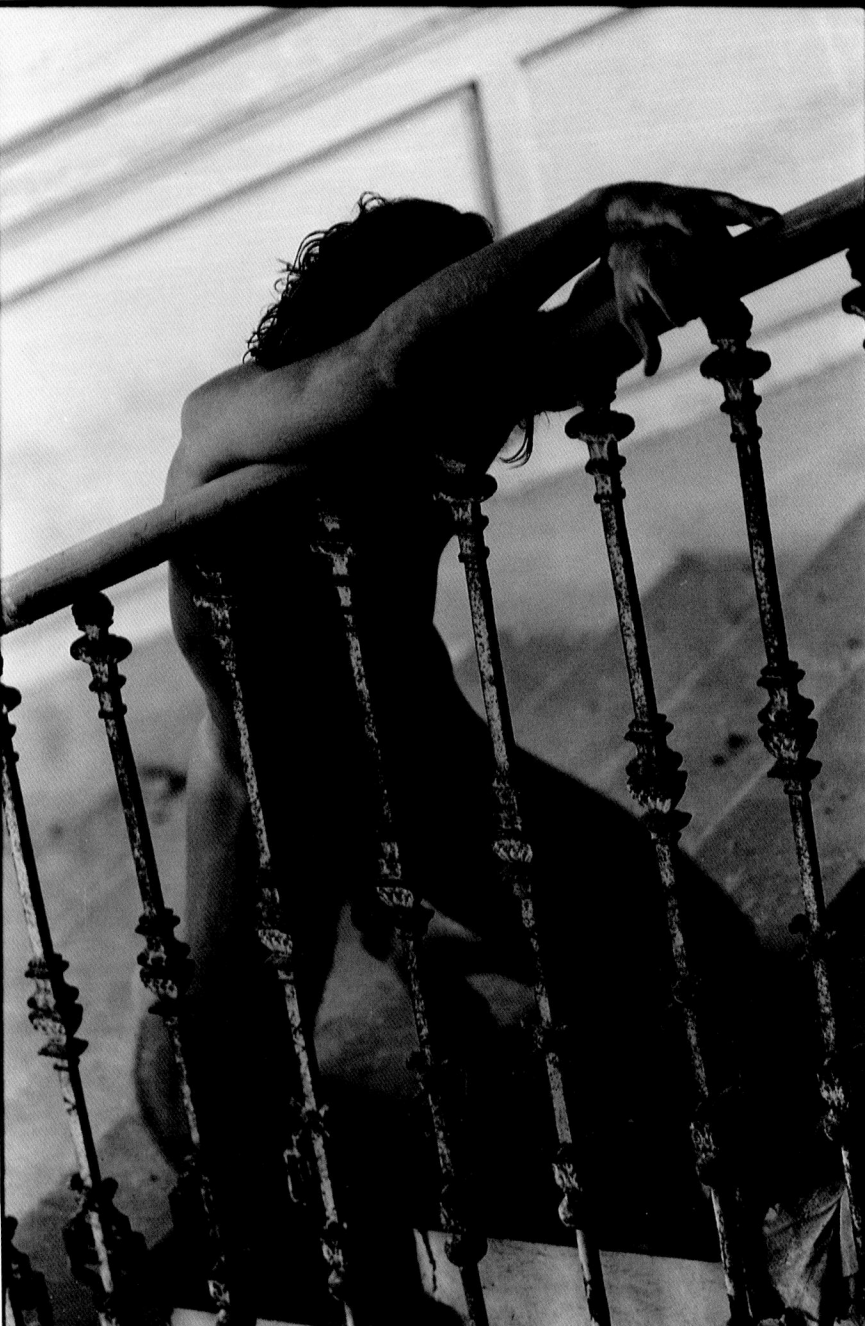

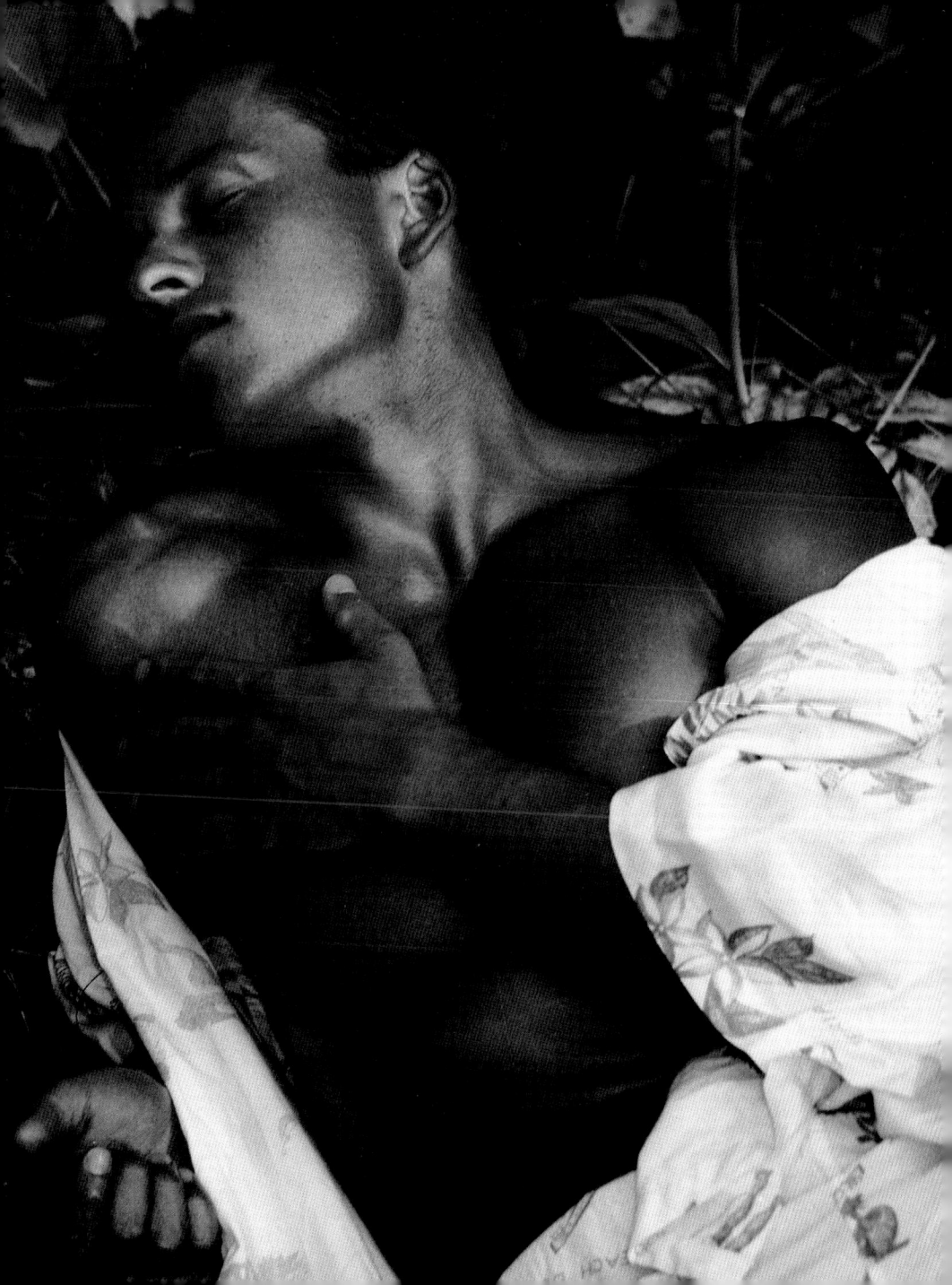

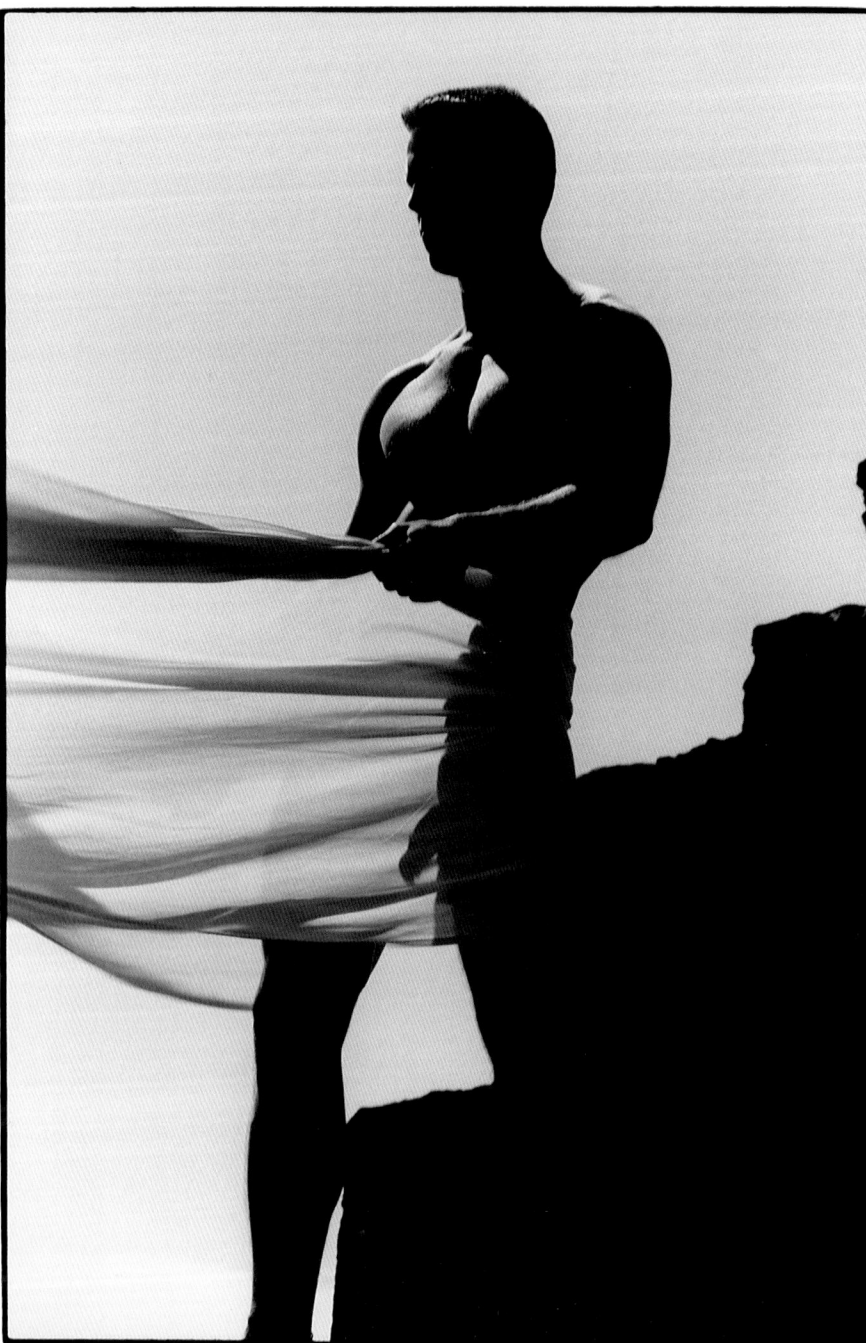

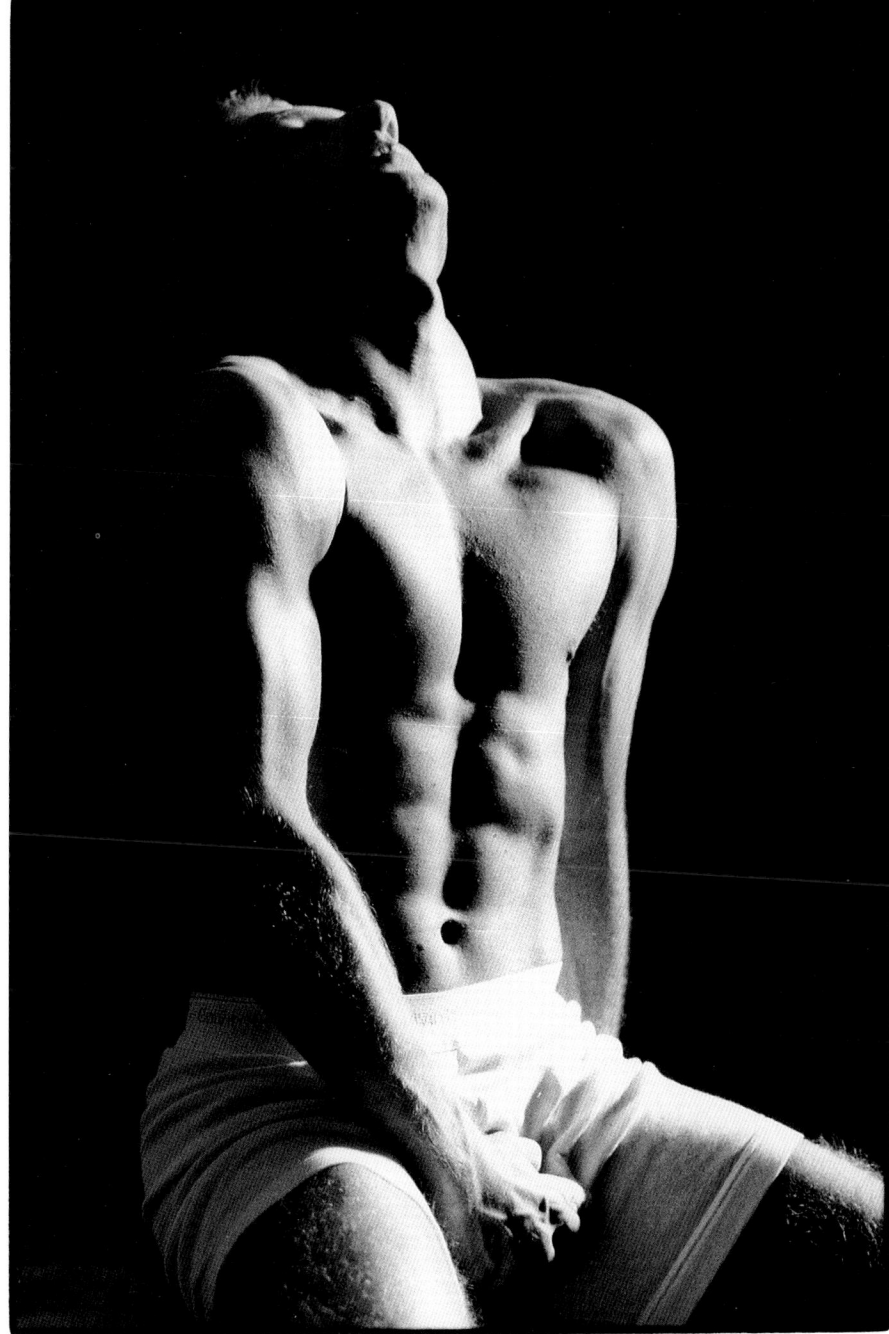

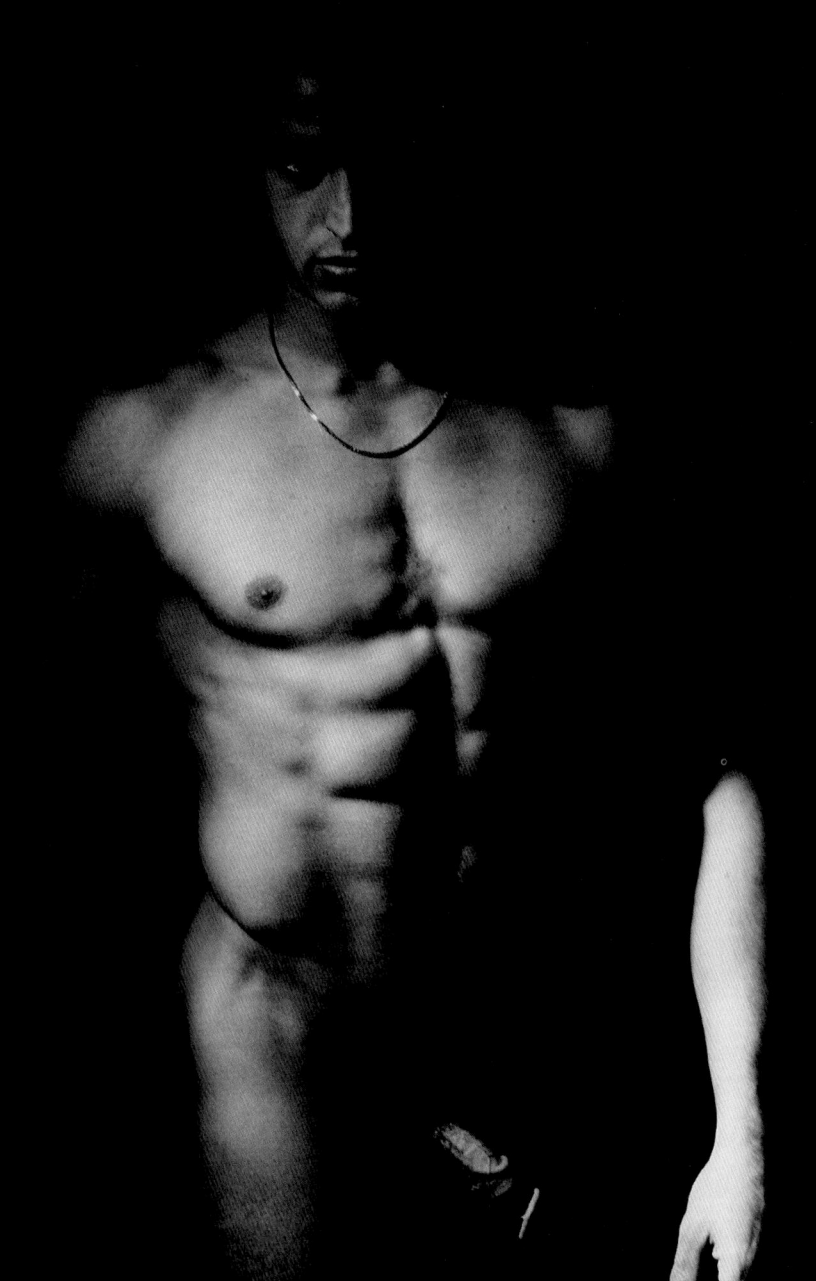

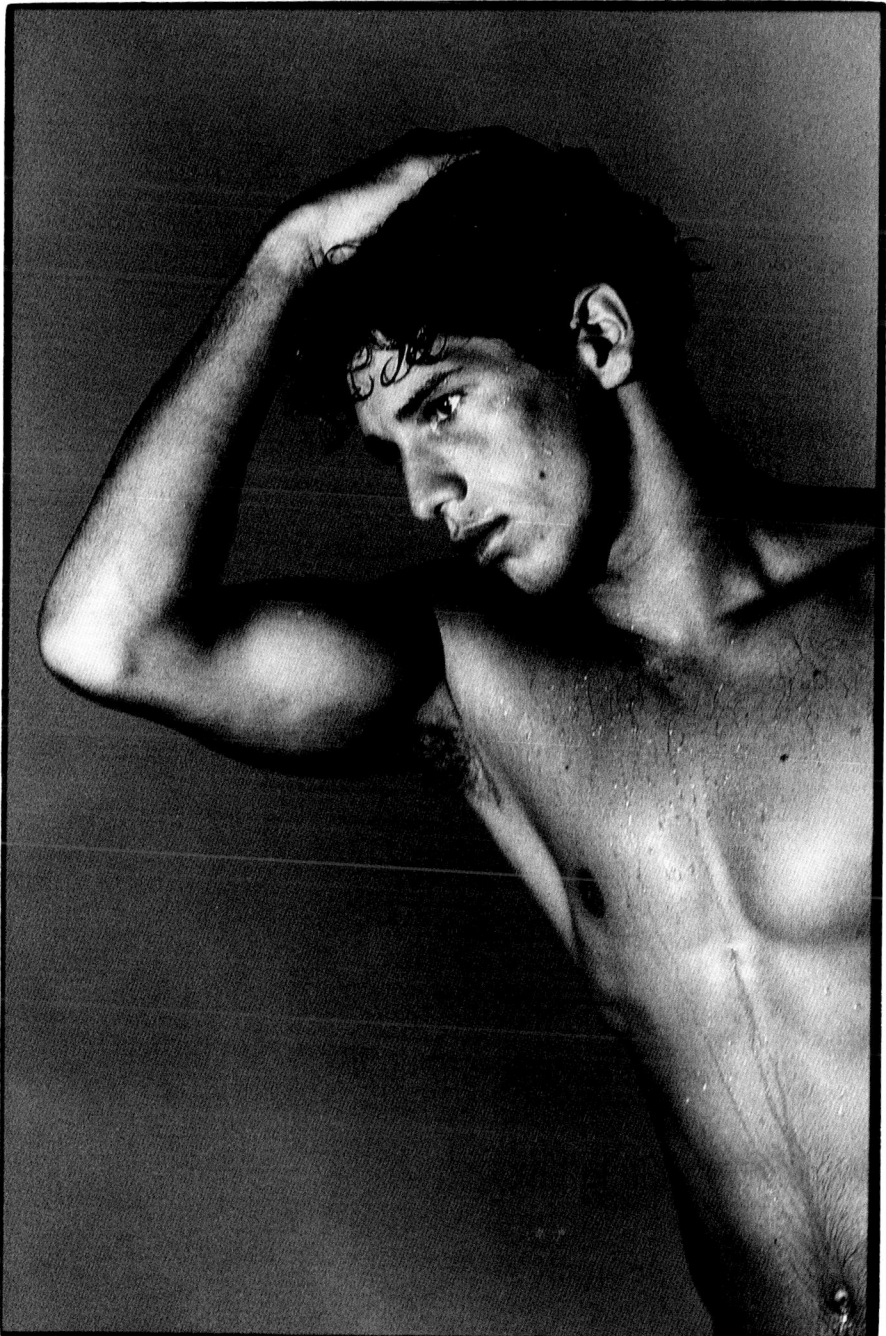

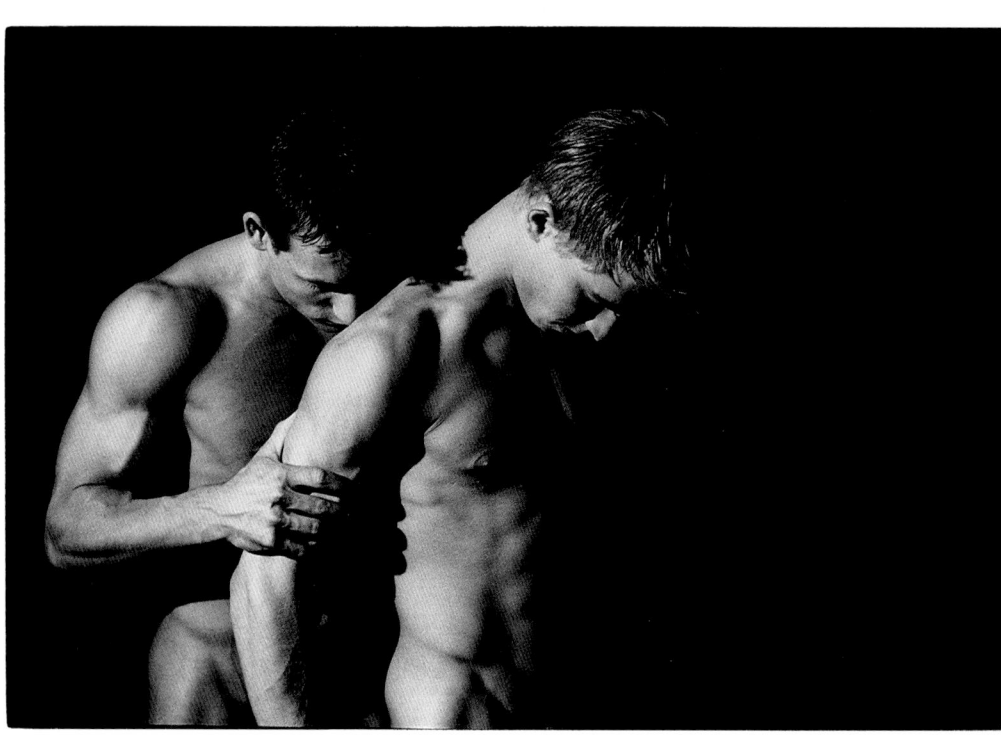

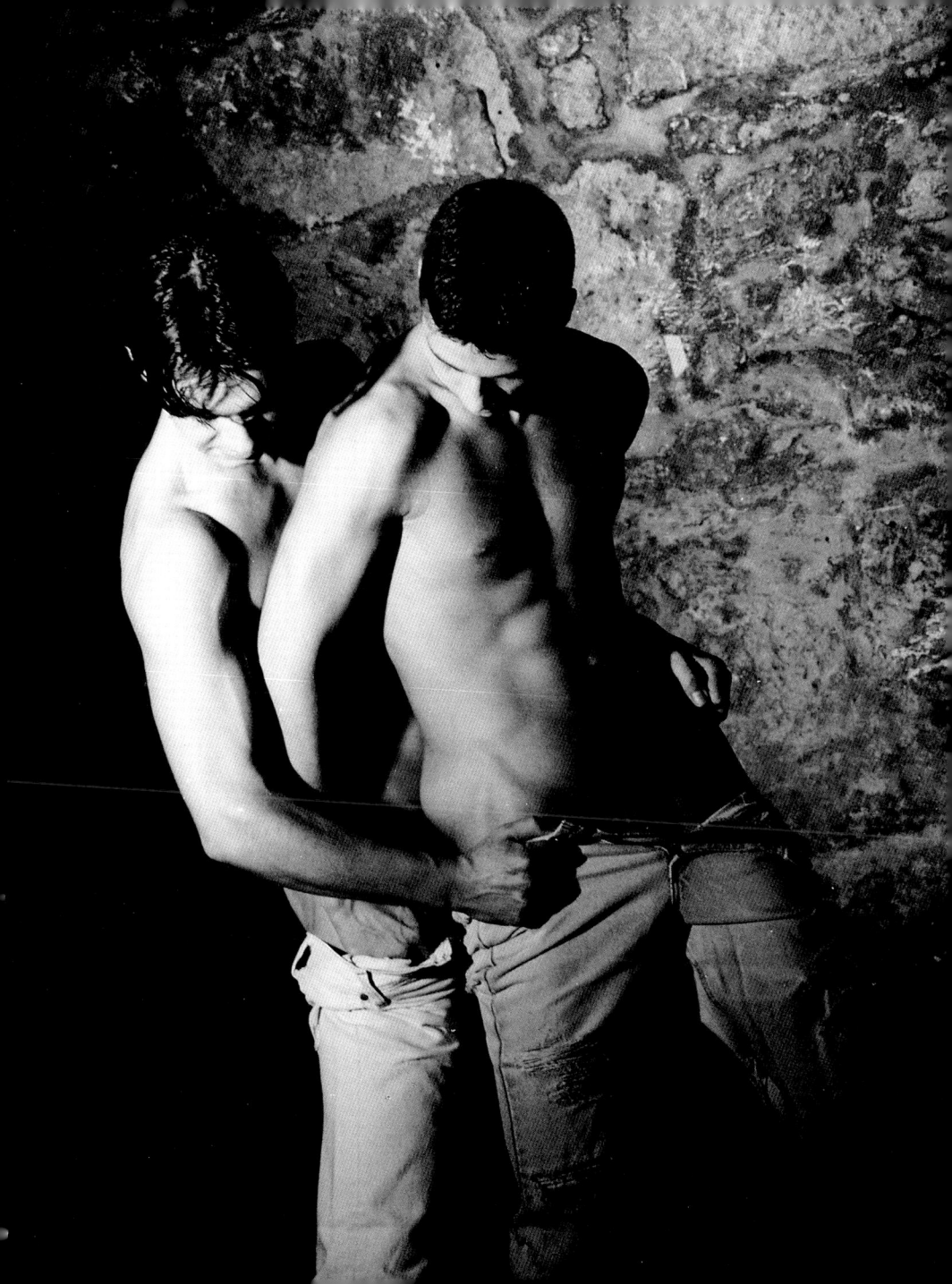

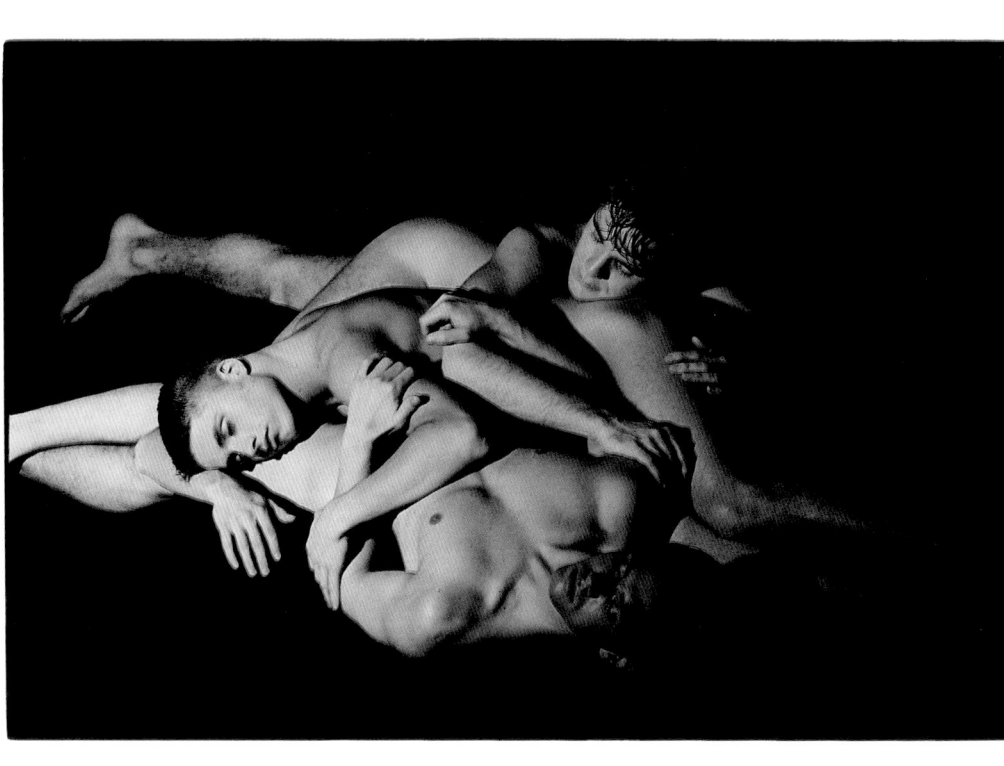

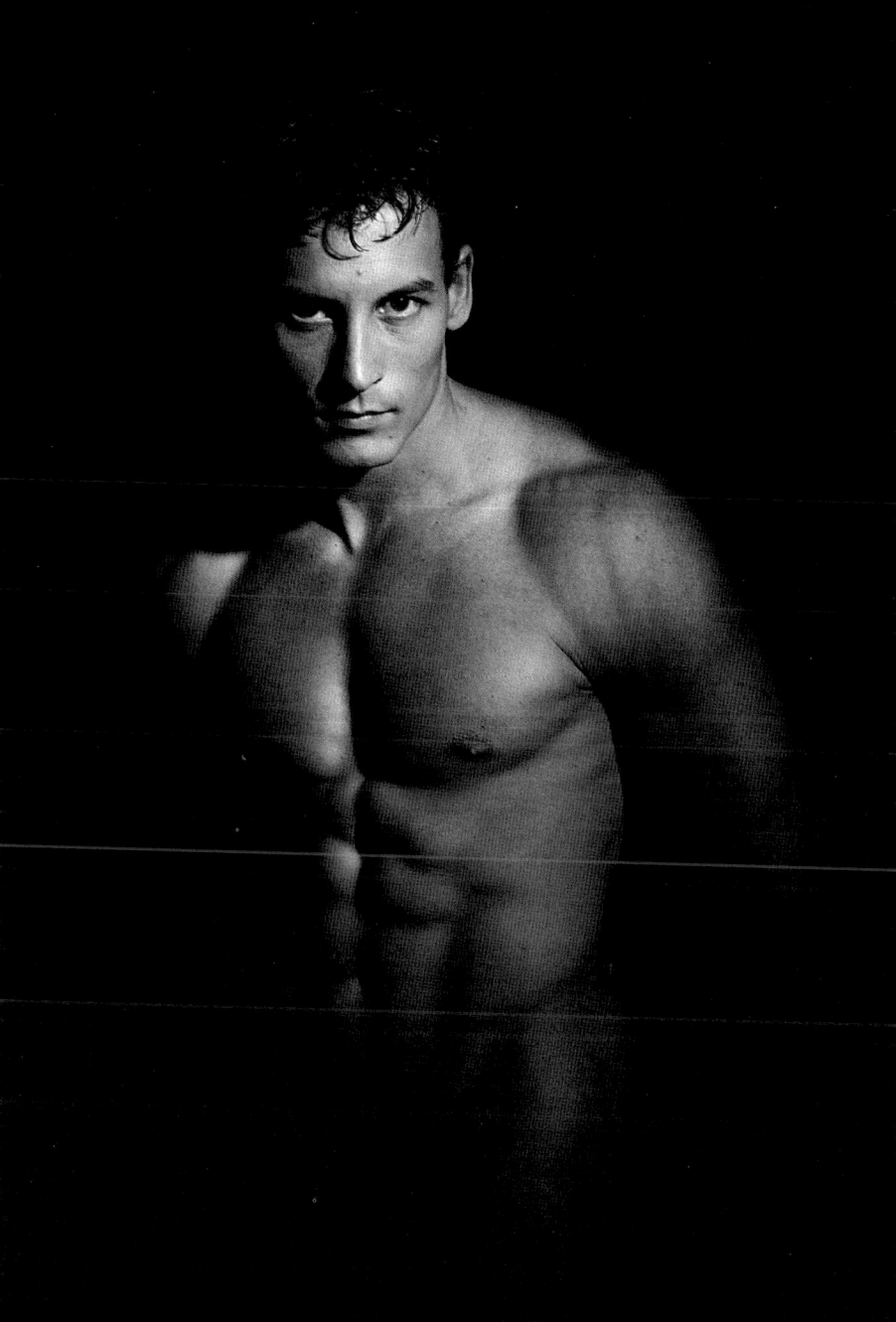

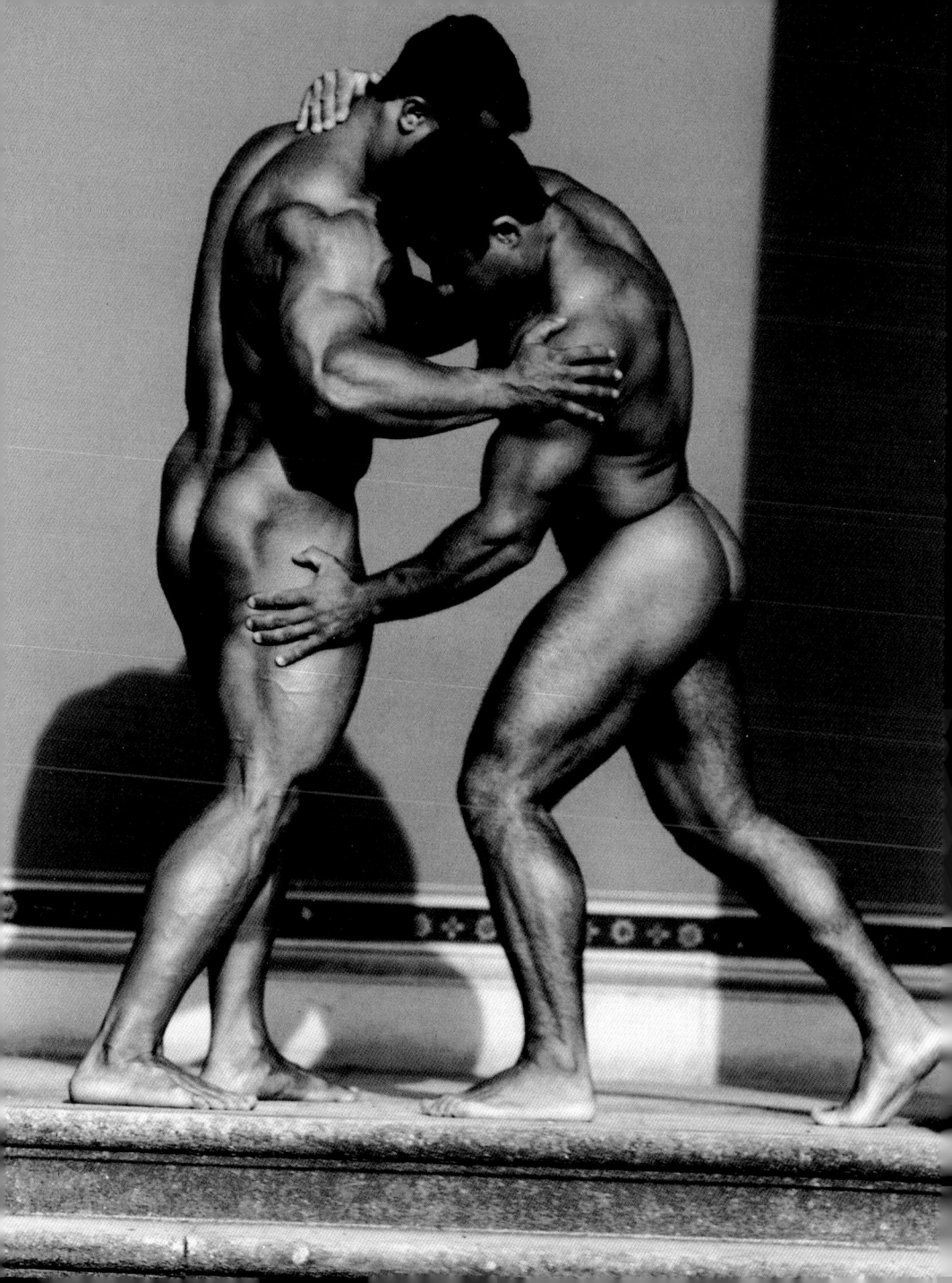

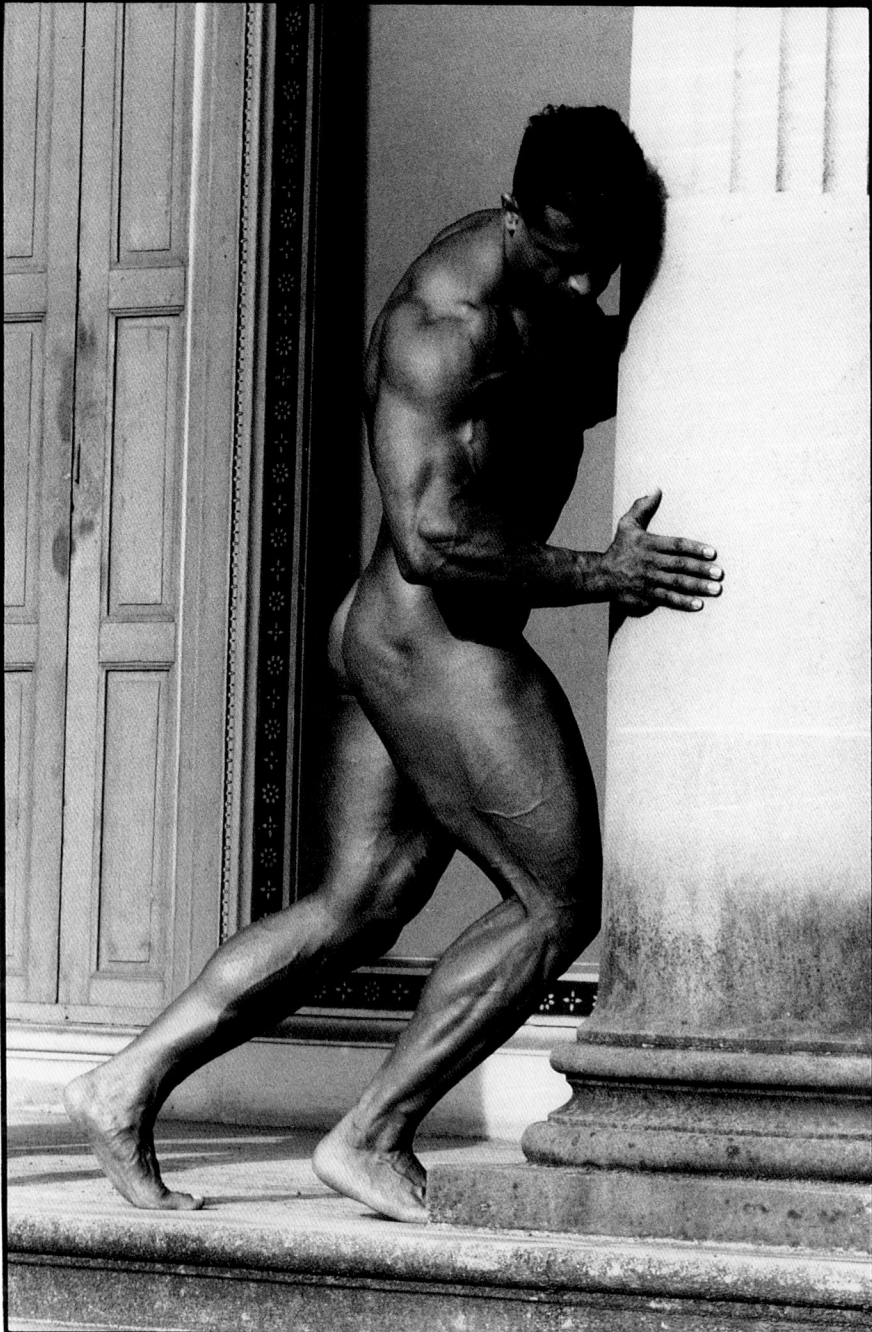

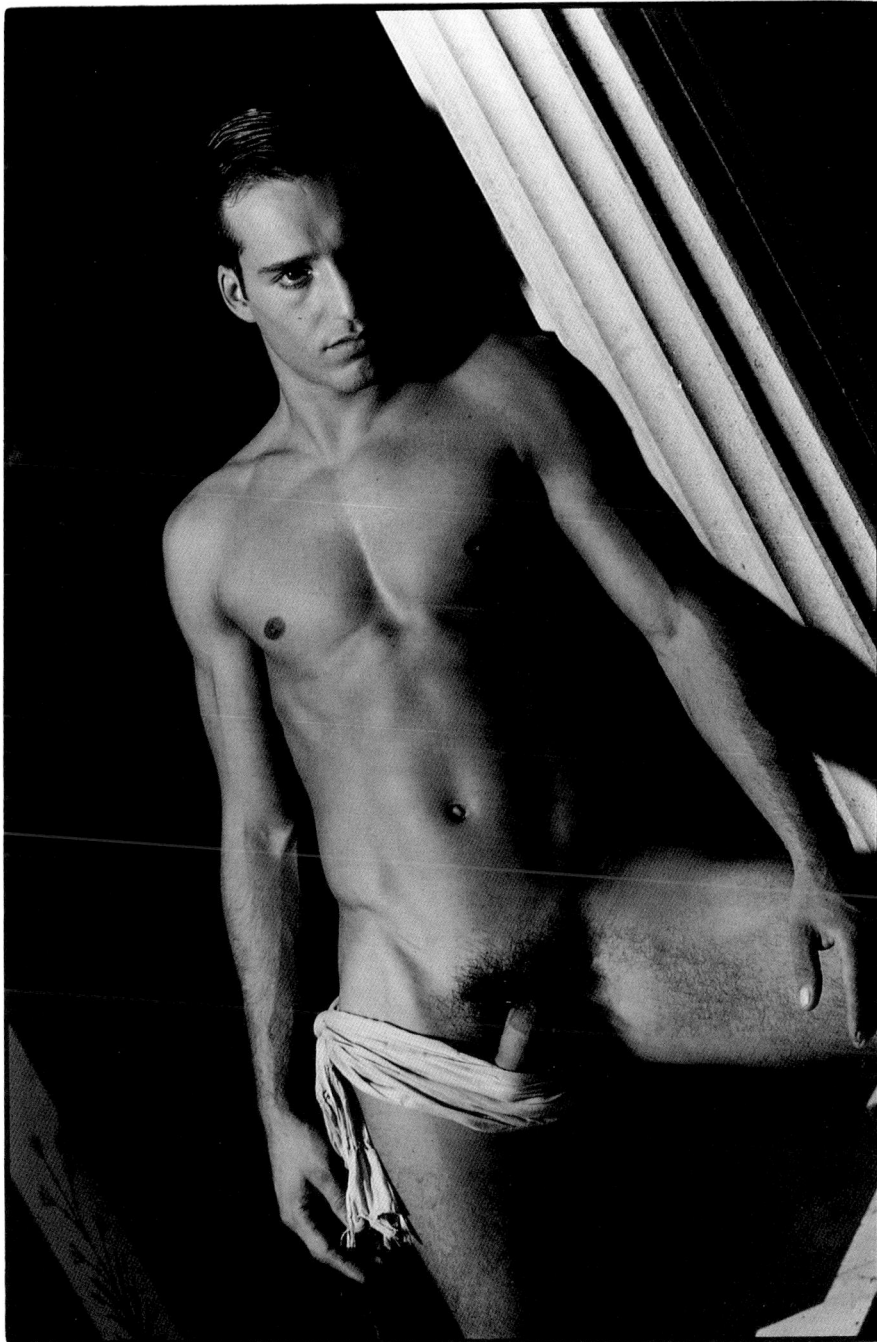

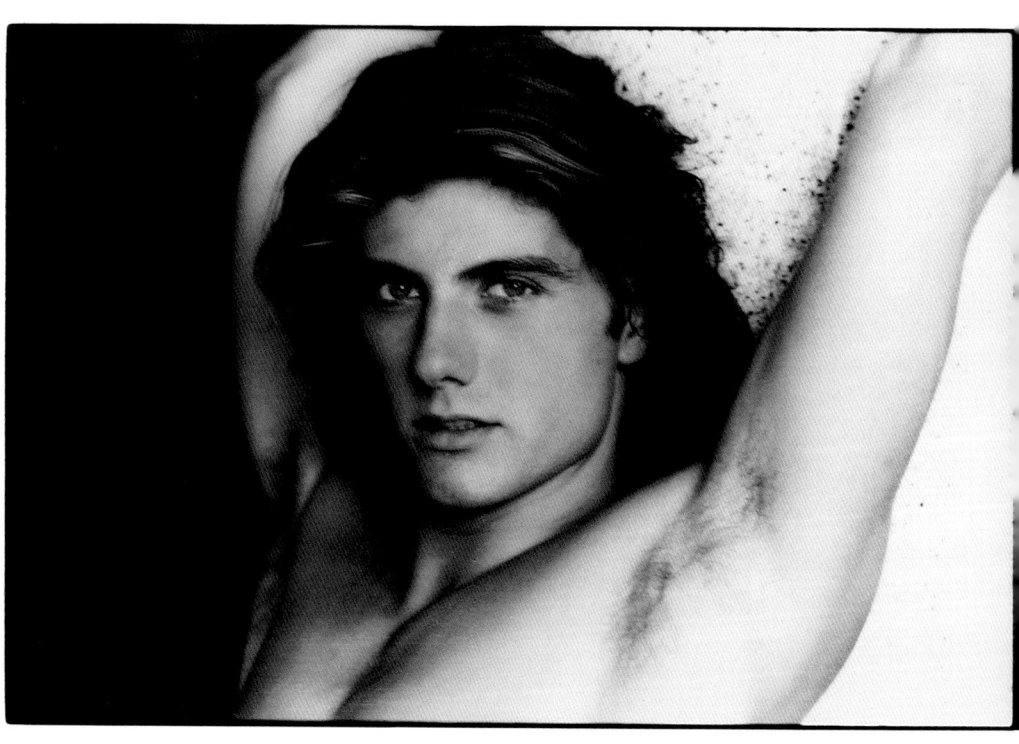

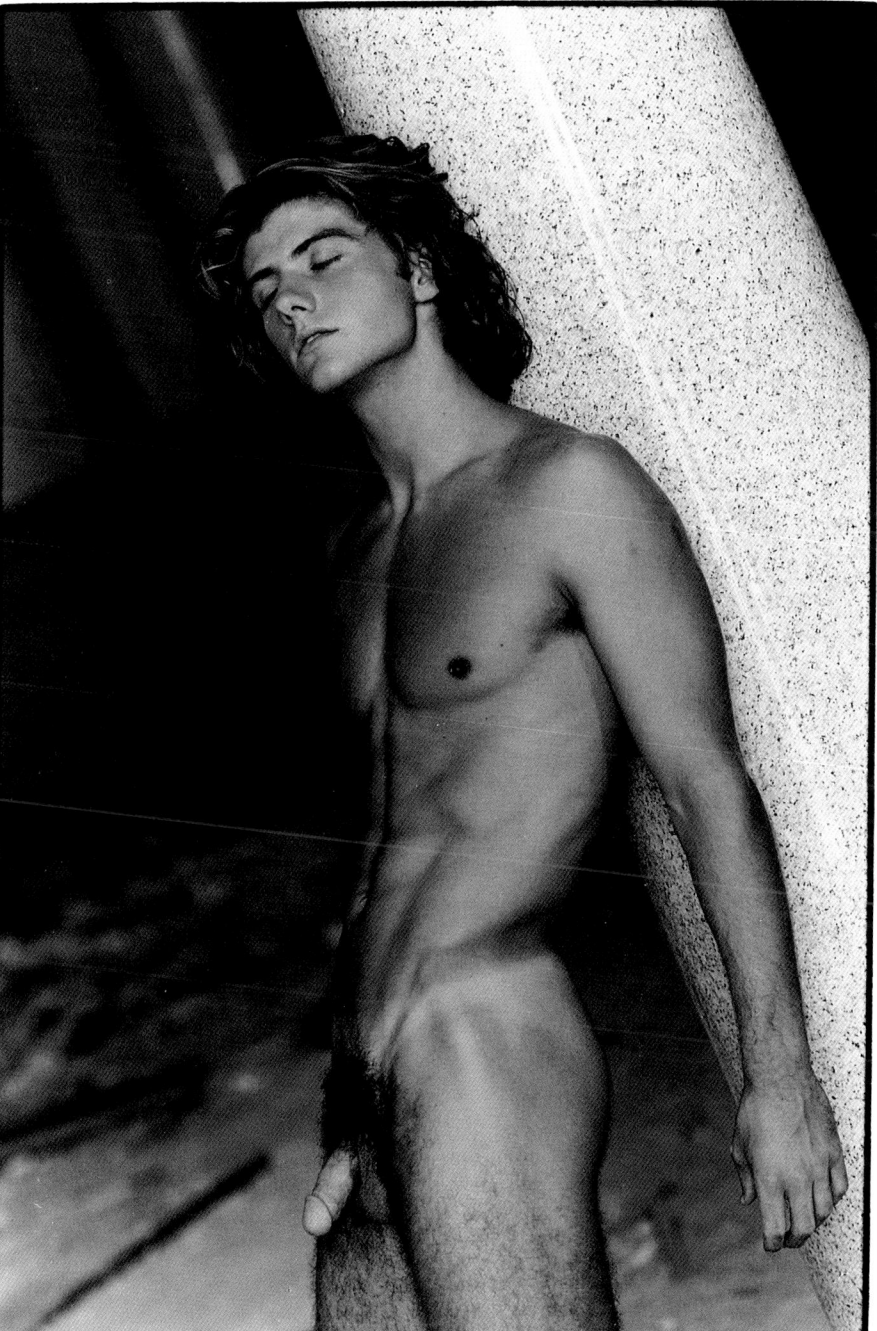

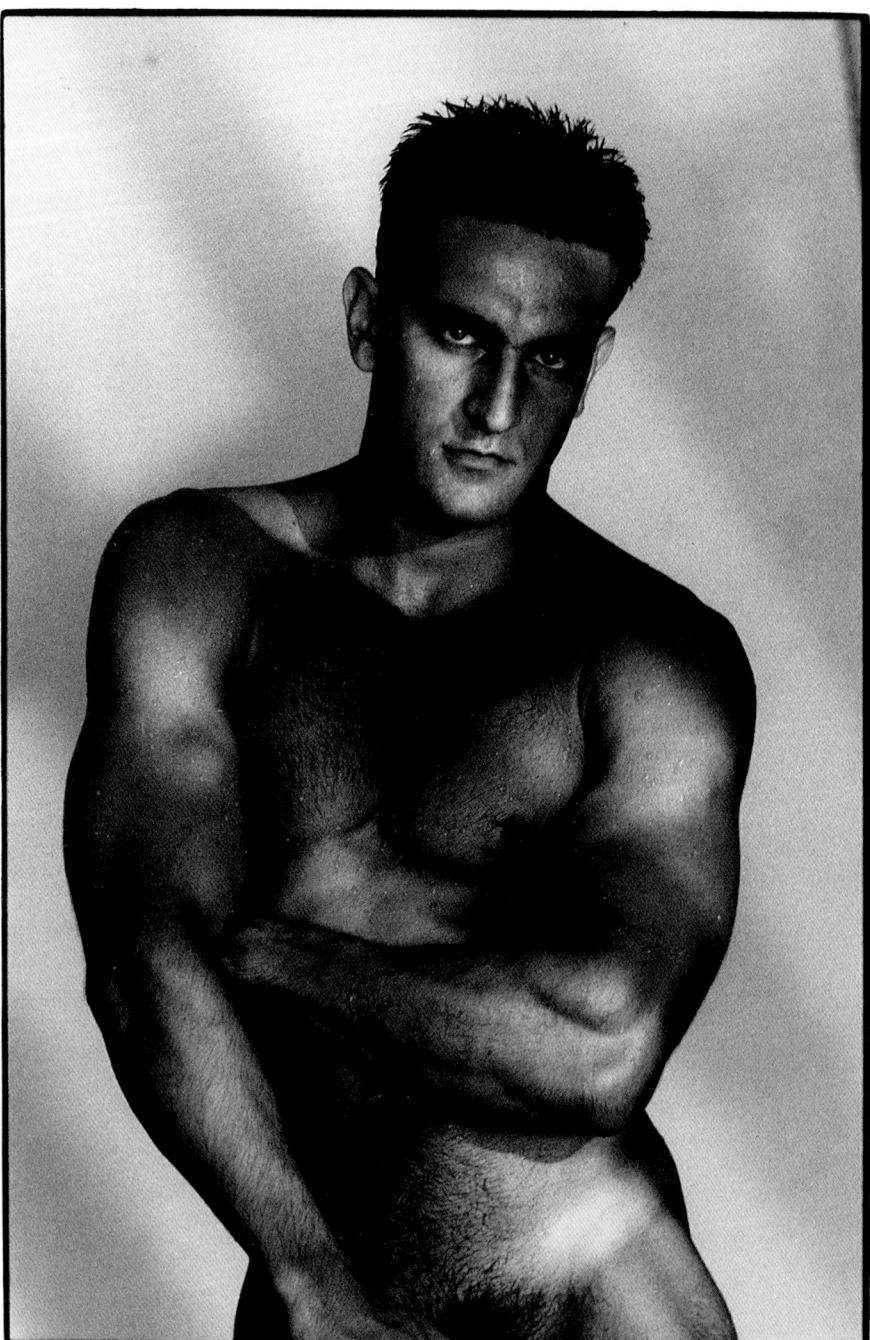

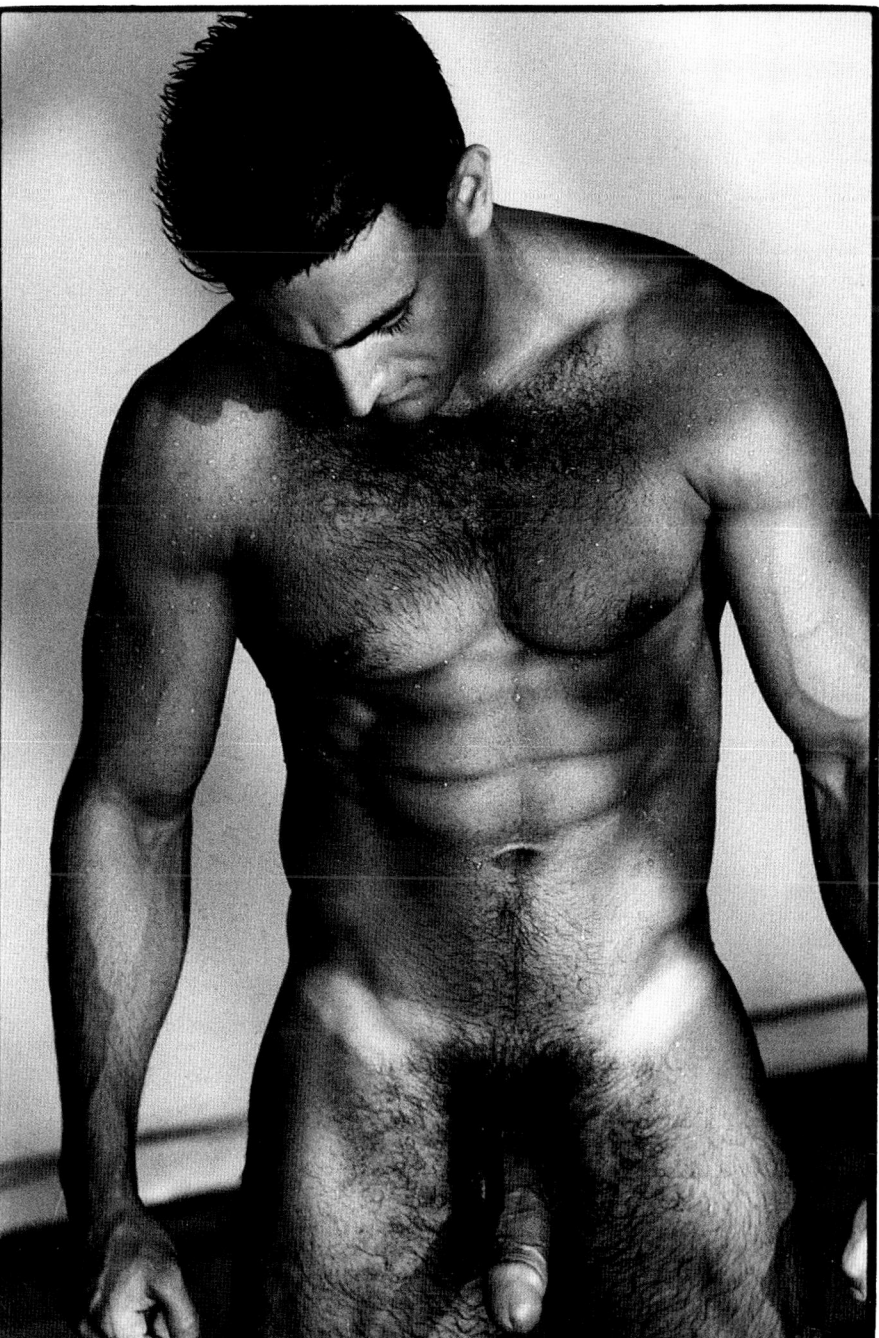

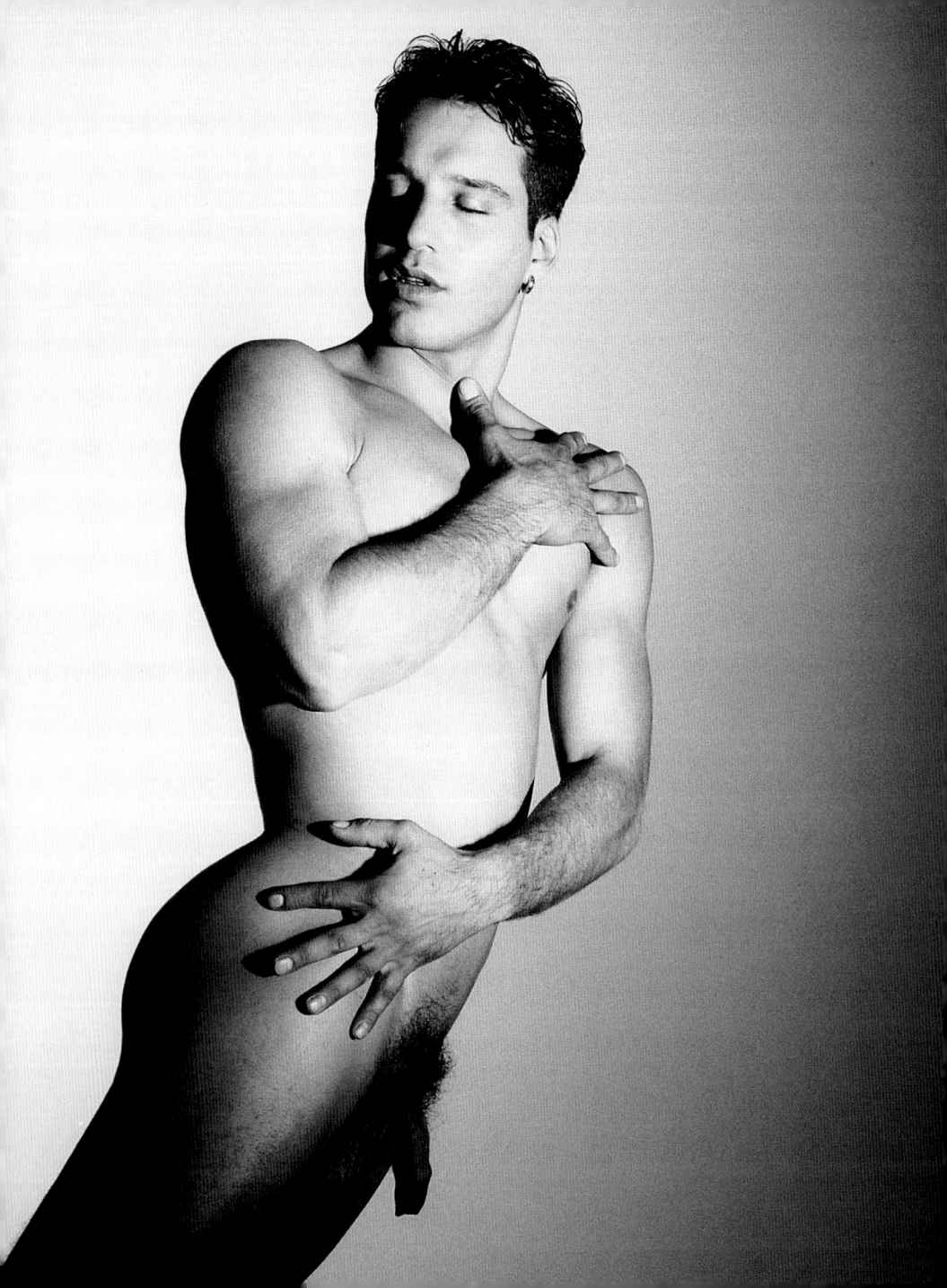

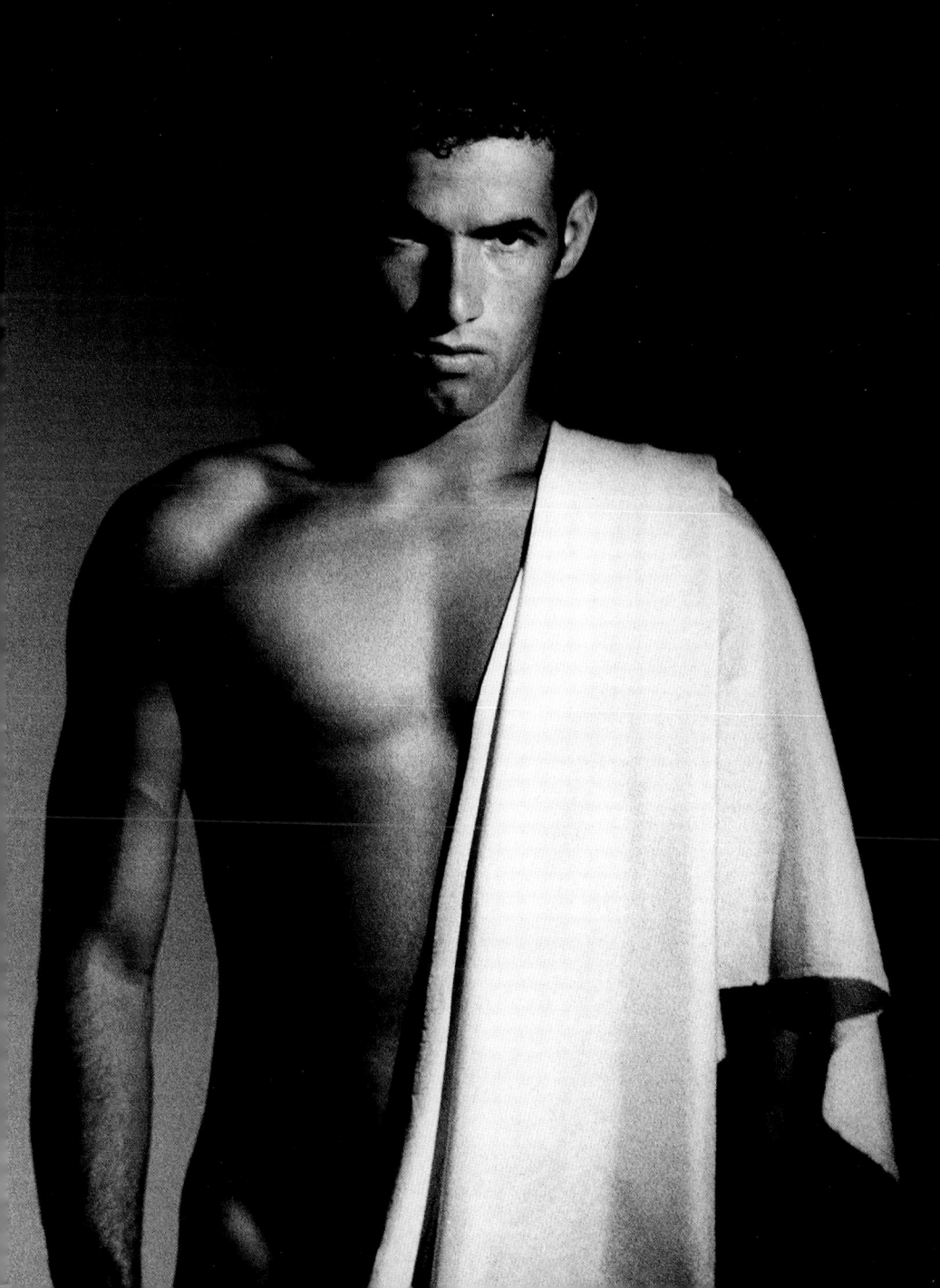

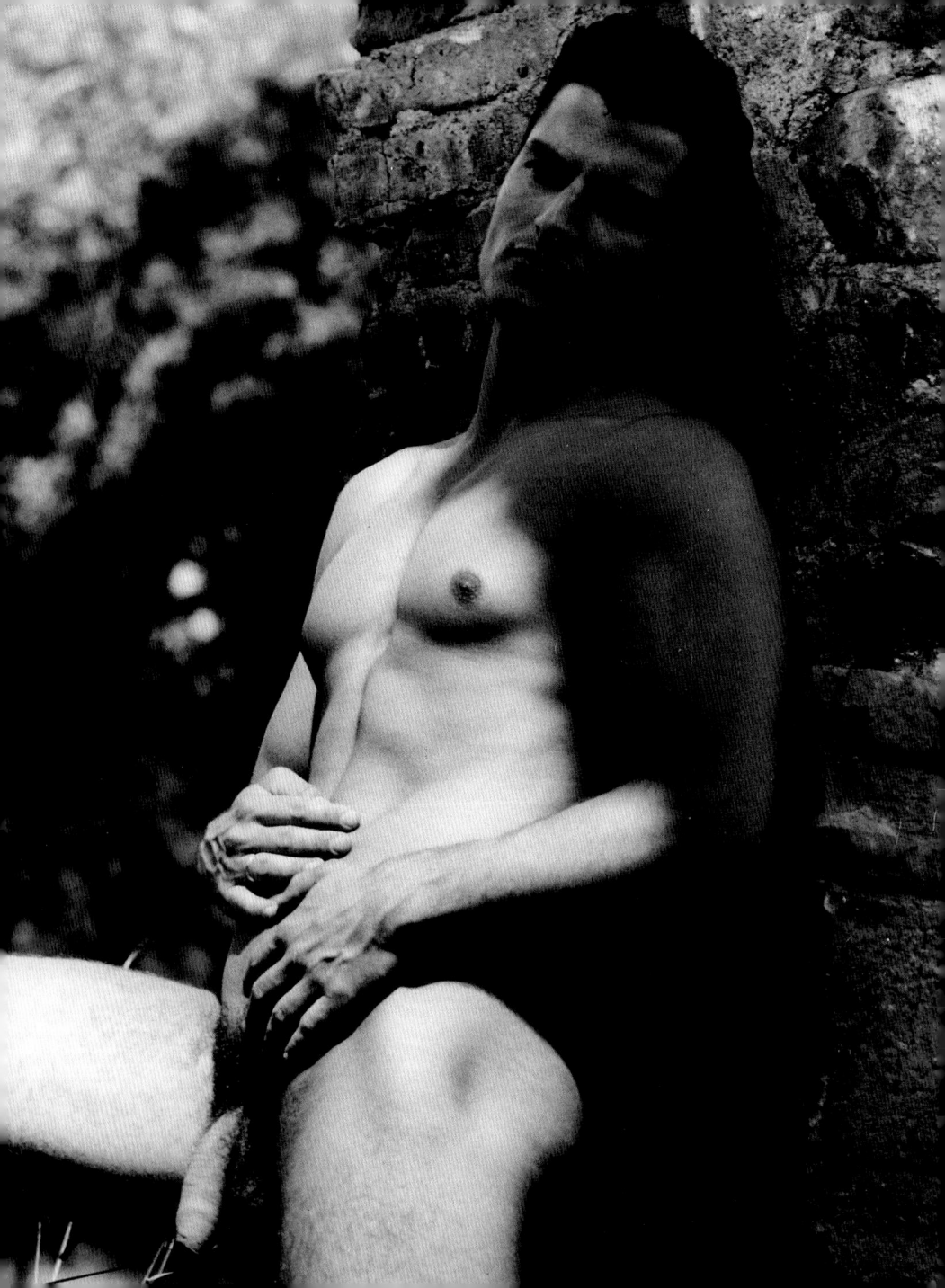

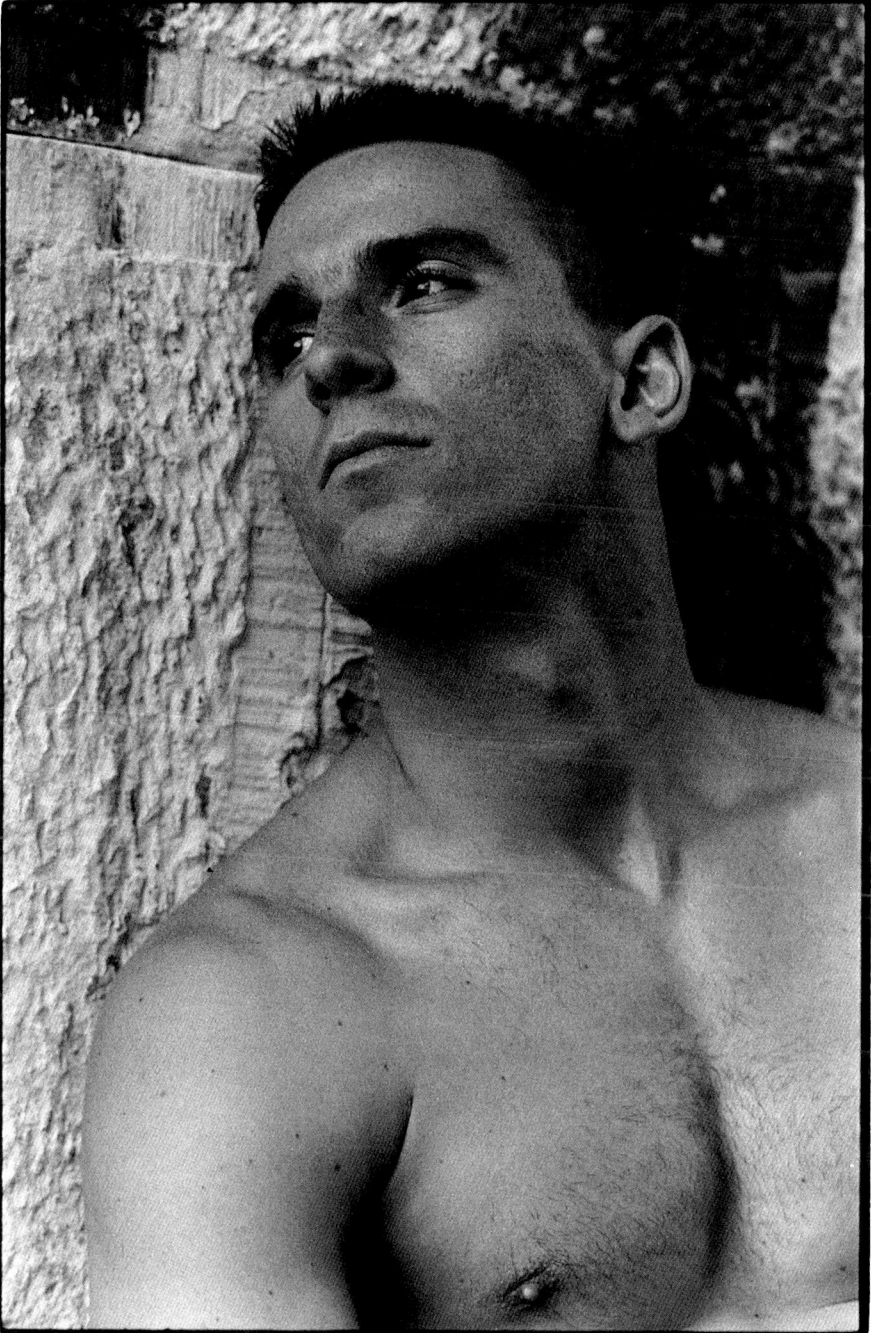

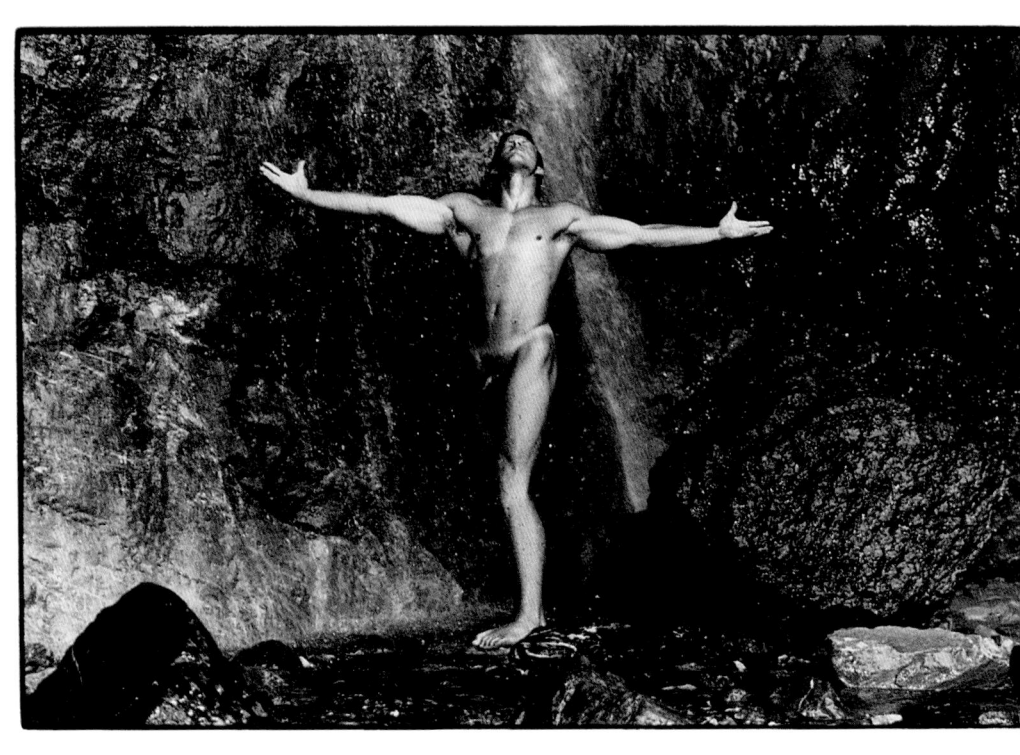

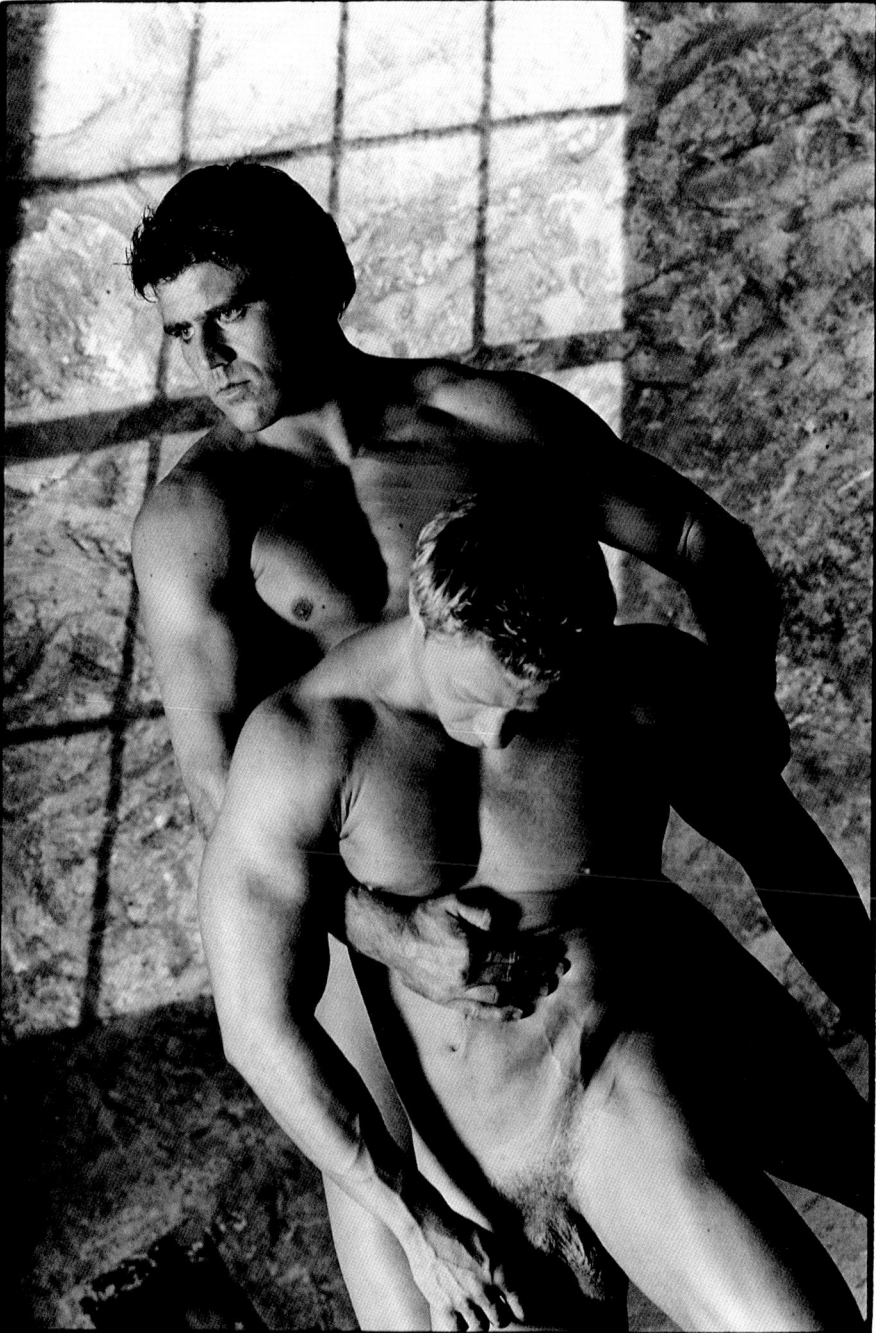

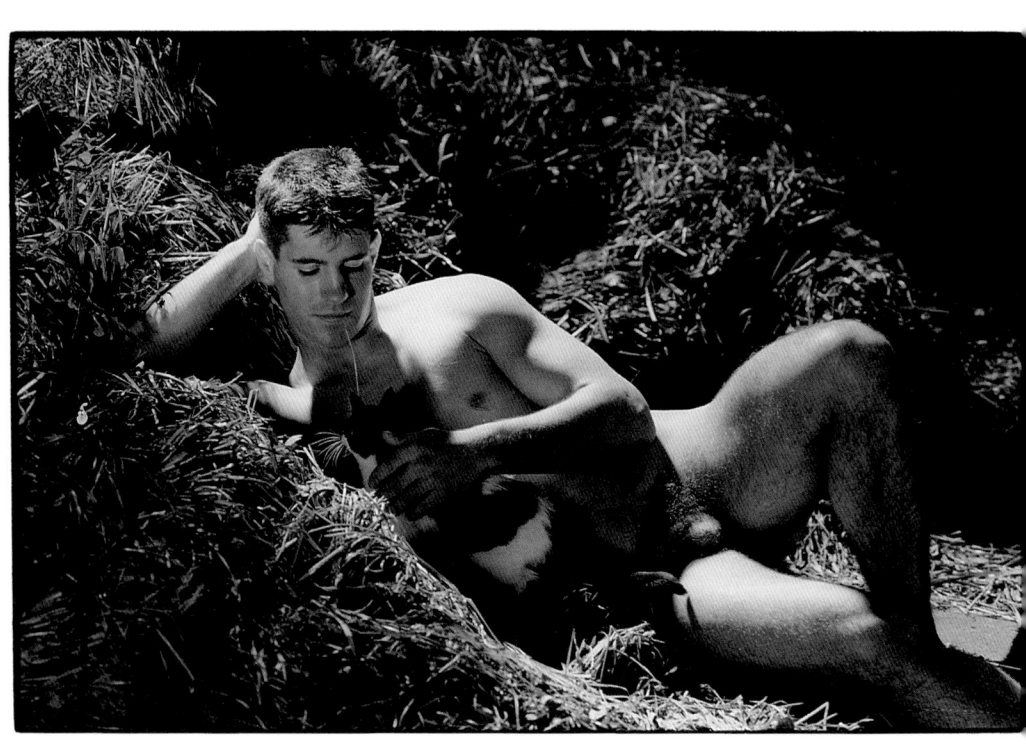

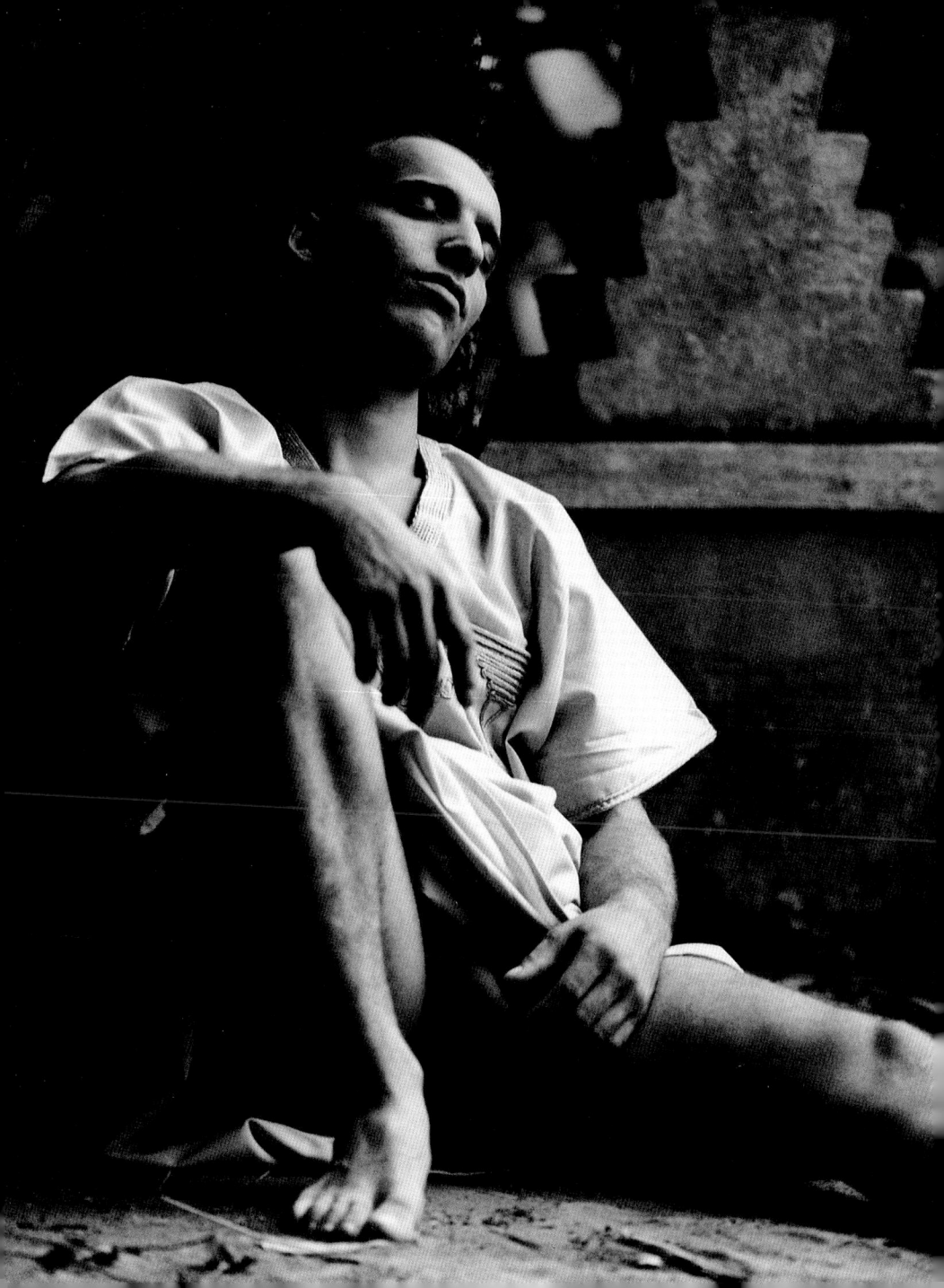

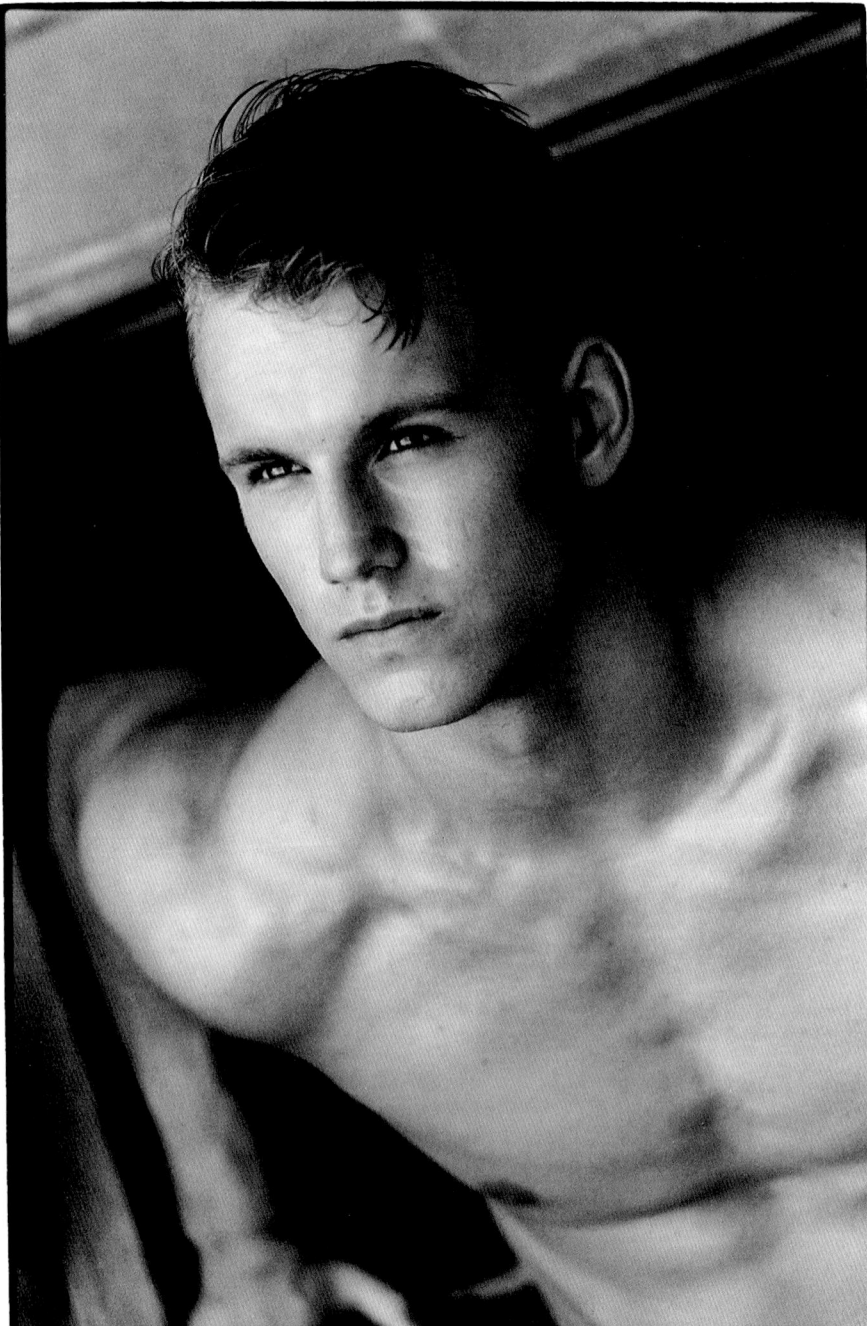

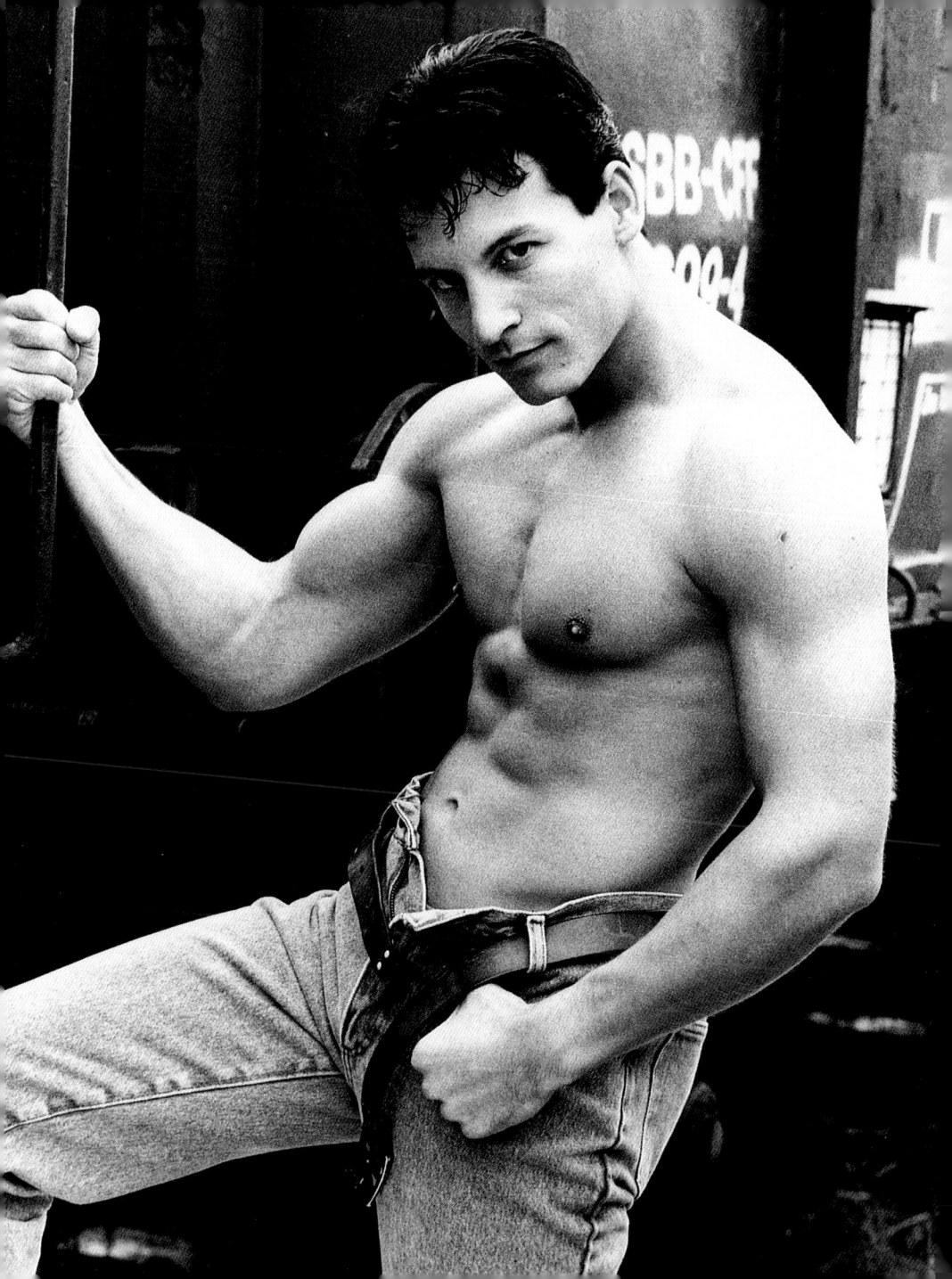

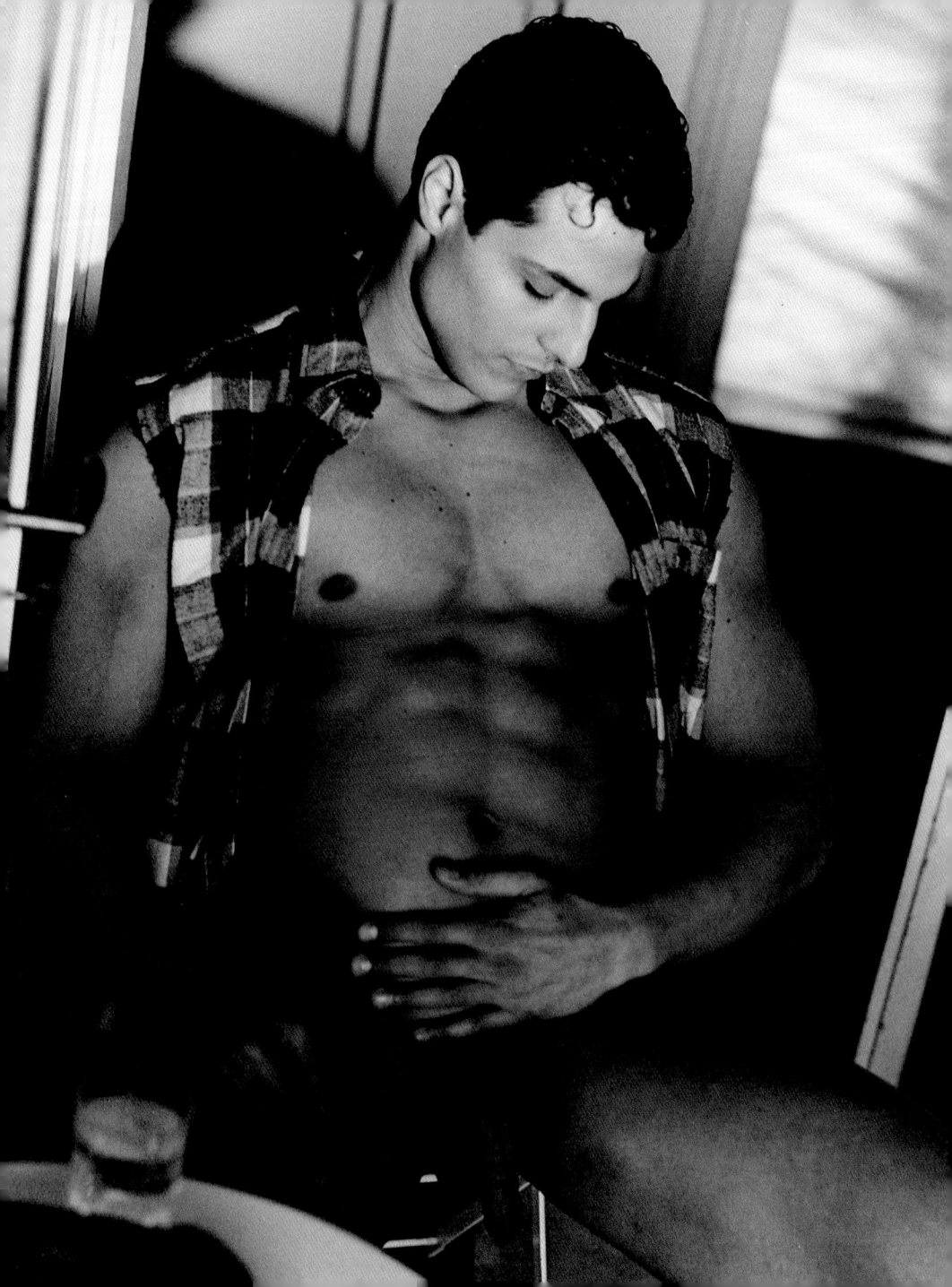

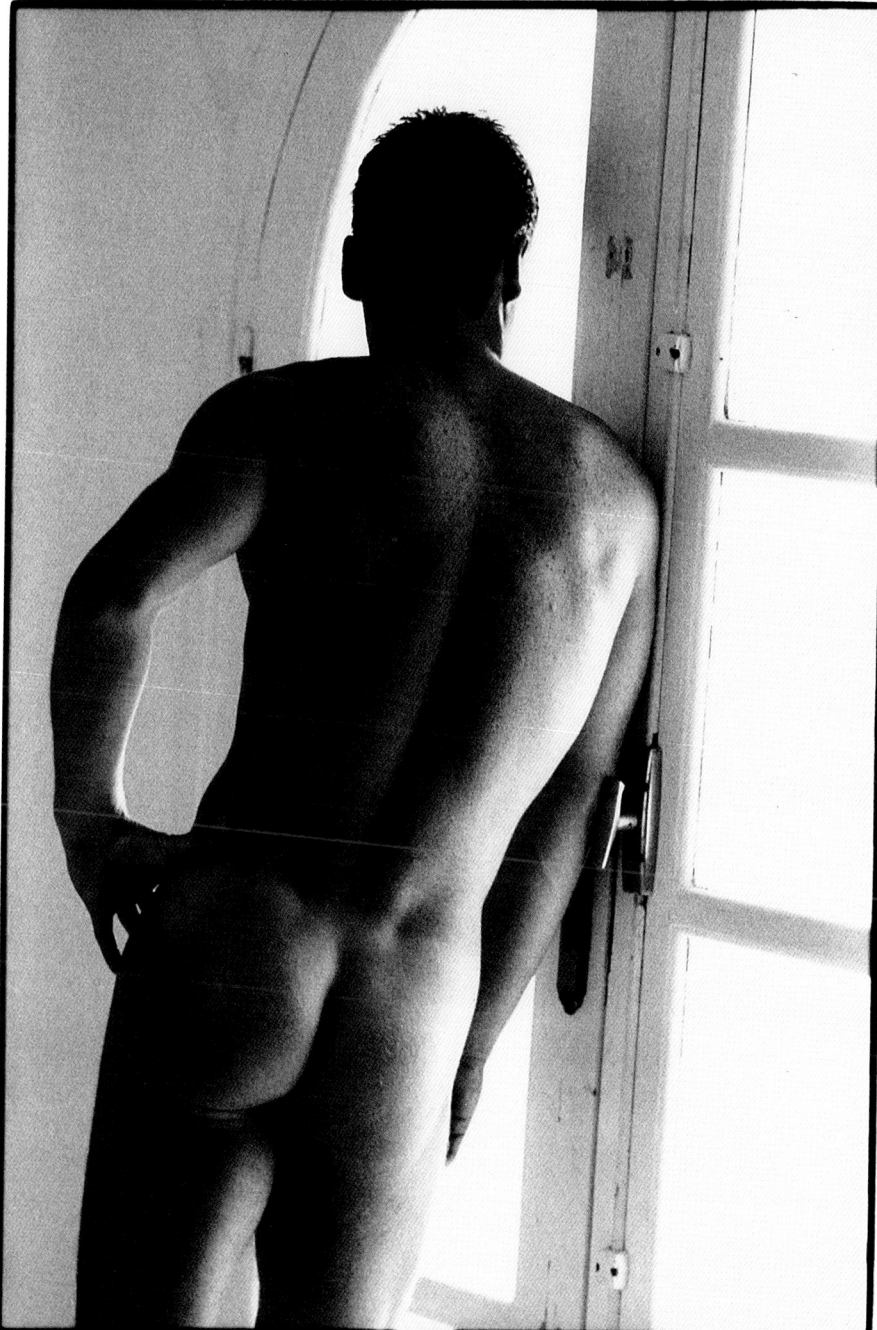

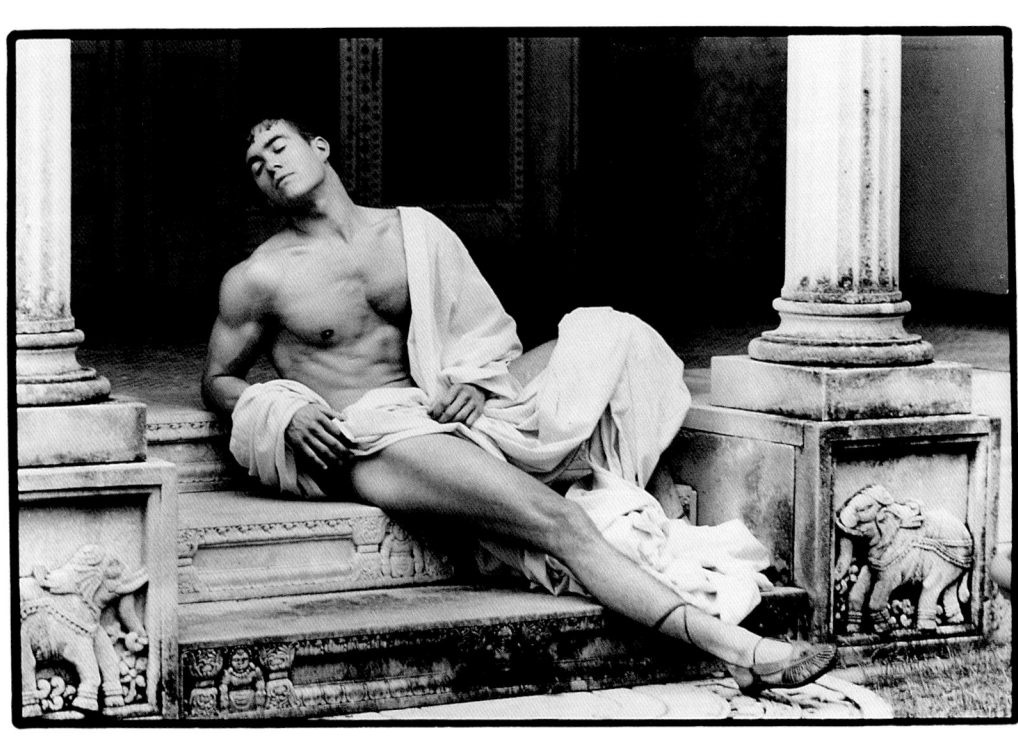

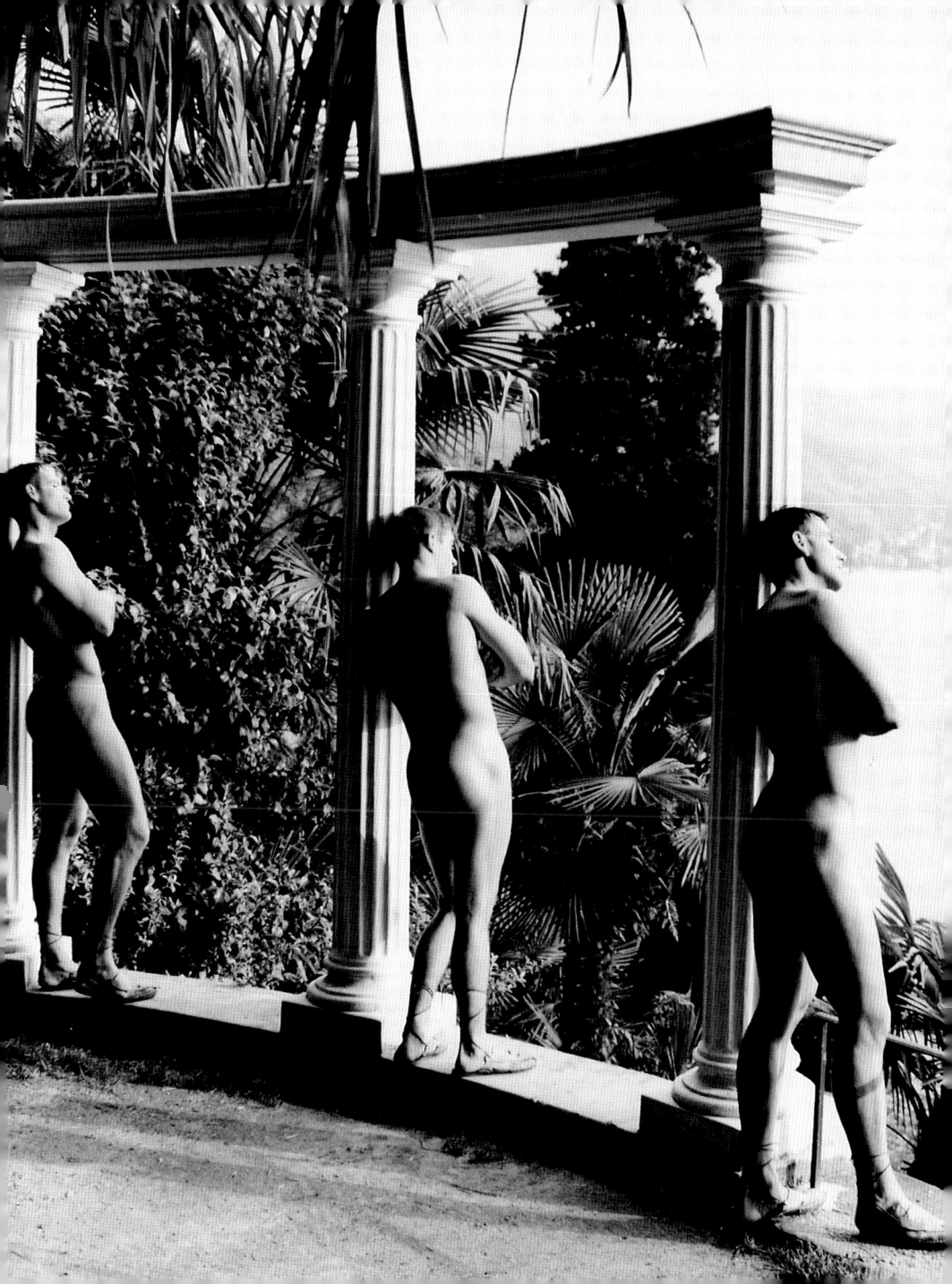

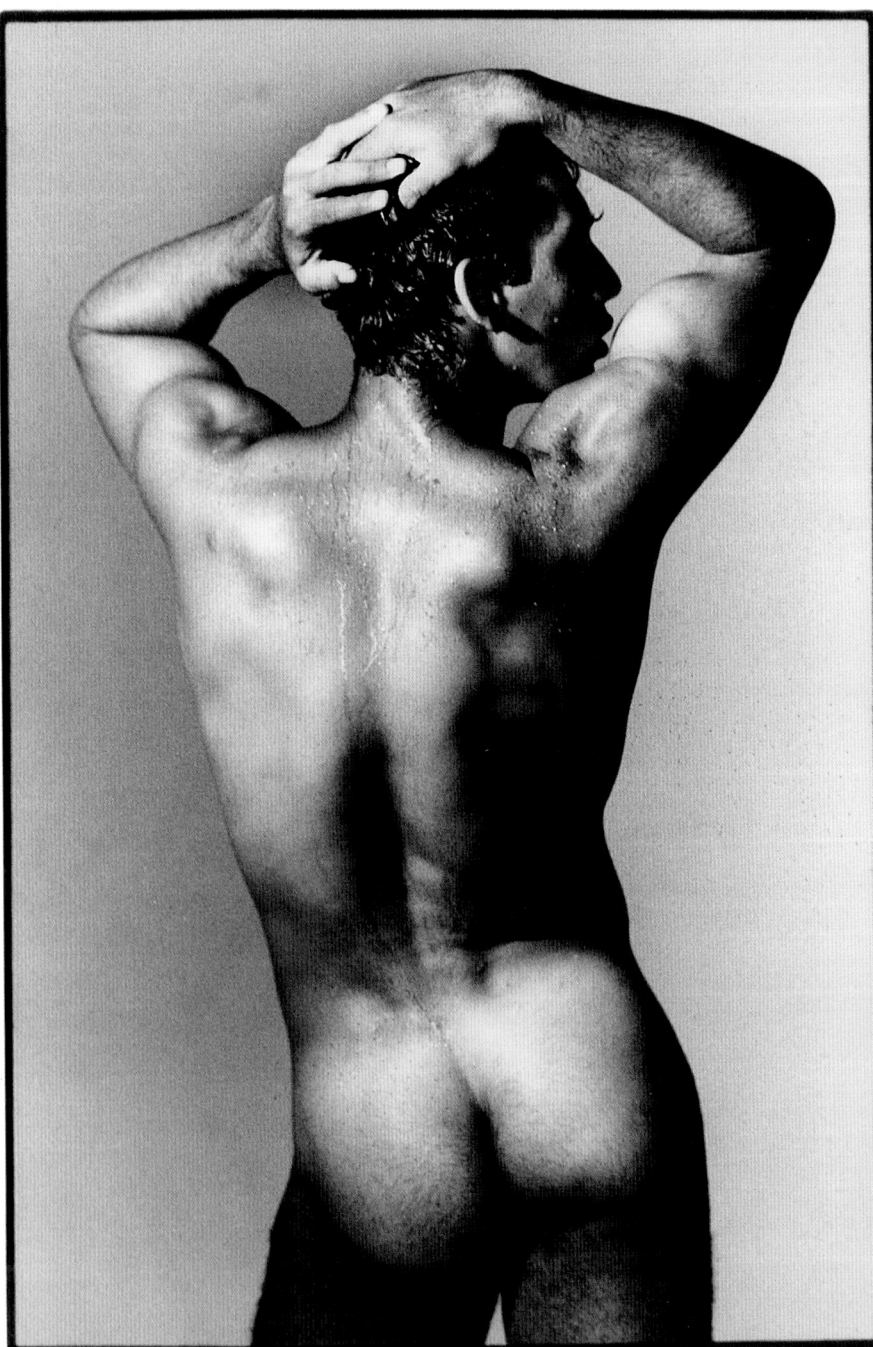

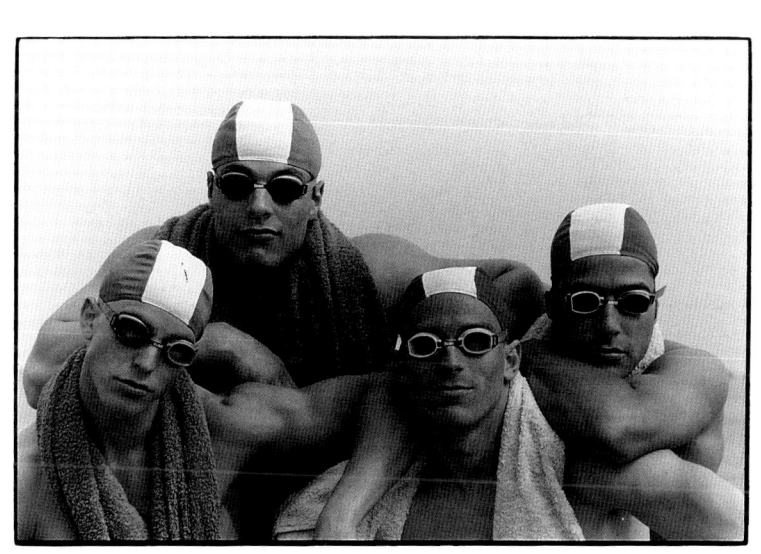

JOSÉ MESSANA

Der 1961 in Zürich/Schweiz geborene José Messana betrachtet die Welt erst nach der harten Ausbildung zum Dolmetscher intensiver durch die Fotolinse. Er wird vom Fotofieber gepackt, das ihn in der Folge nicht mehr losläßt. Und mittlerweile gehört der Autodidakt zu den bekanntesten Aktfotografen Europas. Wer die subtilen Schwarzweißbilder von José Messana betrachtet, spürt die innere Ruhe und die Hingabe, mit der die Bilder inszeniert wurden. Aggressive oder vulgäre Aufnahmen wird man bei diesem Künstler vergebens suchen. Die sanften Töne zwischen dem mythischen Schwarz (typisch für Messana) und dem strahlenden Weiß heben sich so wohltuend von all den grellbunten Bildern ab, die uns tägtäglich begegnen.

Es gibt verschiedene Faktoren, die das Betrachten dieses Buches von José Messsana zu einem wahren Genuß machen. Einer ist sicher die Wahl der Models und der andere ist das geheimnisvolle Spiel von Licht und Schatten. Seine Models bezeichnet Messana als sein größtes Kapital, deshalb betrachtet er sie auch als vollwertige Partner. Kaum verwunderlich, daß Casting und sorgfältige Auswahl der Models einen großen Teil der Produktionsvorbereitungen darstellen. Tatsächlich sucht er teilweise sehr lange nach dem geeigneten Modell für eine von ihm erdachte Bildkomposition.
Fotografieren ist das Beherrschen von Licht. An oberster Stelle aber kommt bei Messana die Wahl des „richtigen" Lichts und dessen Spiel mit dem Schatten. Der Fotograf arbeitet daher bevorzugt im Freien. „Nur mit dem richtigen Licht kann ich meine Ideen adäquat umsetzen..."
Wer seine Bilder betrachtet, versteht, was er damit meint. Beruhigend sind seine Arbeiten allemal.

DIETER M. STEGER

José Messana was born in Zurich, Switzerland in 1961 and didn't begin to view the world intensively through a camera lens until he'd completed the difficult training needed to become an interpreter. He then caught the photographic bug with a vengeance, and still has it. The self-taught camera virtuoso has become one of Europe's best-known photographers of nudes. Looking at Jose Messana's subtle black-and-white pictures makes the viewer aware of the inner peace and devotion that went into their creation. There is no point in looking for either aggressive or vulgar pictures in this artist's work. The soft tones between the almost mystic black (typical for Messana) and the radiant white are delightfully different to all the brightly coloured pictures with which we are all daily confronted.

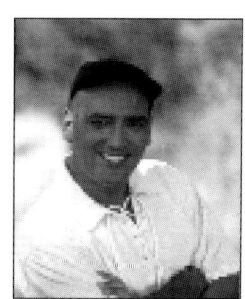

There are a number of factors making looking through this book by José Messana a genuine pleasure. One is most certainly the choice of model and another the cryptic contrasting of light and shade. Messana describes his models as his greatest capital, which is why he sees them as full partners and not mere objects. It's hardly surprising that casting and model selection make up a large part of production preparation. He spends a great deal of time finding suitable models for his pictorial compositions.

Photography is mastery of light conditions. But Messana places greatest emphasis on choosing the right light and its interplay with shade, which is why he prefers working in the open. I can only realize my ideas given the right light.

Every viewer understands exactly what he means. His compositions always achieve a soothing effect.

DIETER M. STEGER

Acknowledgements:
Special thanks to Patrizio Di Renzo for his marvellous prints, and to my primo uomo Mikel who is a neverending source of inspiration.

Many thanks also to all other models:
Dave, Daniele, Stephan B., Martin Sch., Michi, Jovi, Roger, Martin R., Stephan E., Claudio, Markus A., Delfrance, Paolo, Marco Aurelio, Peter, Andy, Haji, Clemens, Muammer, Raffi, Alessandro, Steve, Roman, Frédéric, Markus Sch., Hardy and Donatello. – Merci. J.M.

Limited edition prints from this books are available. For information write to:
Edition Ars Photographica, c/o M. Müller, Altenhofstrasse 45, CH-8008 Zürich, Switzerland.

© 1996, Bruno Gmünder Verlag
PO Box 11 07 29
10837 Berlin
Germany
Phone: ++49 (30) 615 00 30

Photographs Copyright © 1996,
José Messana, Switzerland

Lithography:
Rainbow Graphics
Production & Layout:
Michael Taubenheim
Printing: Heenemann
Printed in Germany
ISBN 3-86187-074-6

BITTE FORDERN SIE UNSEREN BILDPROSPEKT AN!
DEMANDEZ NOTRE CATALOGUE ILLUSTRÉ!
PLEASE ASK FOR OUR FREE MAIL-ORDER CATALOGUE!

Bisher sind in der Reihe EDITION EUROS erschienen:

EDITION EUROS Nr 1
Clifford Baker
15 x 19 cm, 60 Seiten, ca 50 Bildtafeln.
Druck in Duoton, Hardcover.
ISBN 3-86187-061-4
22,80 DM

EDITION EUROS Nr 4
Andrew Melick
15 x 19 cm, 60 Seiten, ca 50 Bildtafeln.
Druck in Duoton, Hardcover.
ISBN 3-86187-073-8
22,80 DM

EDITION EUROS Nr 2
Mark Brickell
15 x 19 cm, 60 Seiten, ca 50 Bildtafeln.
Druck in Duoton, Hardcover.
ISBN 3-86187-062-2
22,80 DM

EDITION EUROS Nr 5
José Messana
15 x 19 cm, 60 Seiten, ca 50 Bildtafeln.
Druck in Duoton, Hardcover.
ISBN 3-86187-074-6
22,80 DM

EDITION EUROS Nr 3
Benno Thoma
15 x 19 cm, 60 Seiten, ca 50 Bildtafeln.
Druck in Duoton, Hardcover.
ISBN 3-86187-072-X
22,80 DM

EDITION EUROS Nr 6
Desert Patrol, Photographs by Dook
15 x 19 cm, 80 Seiten, ca 87 Bildtafeln.
Druck in Duoton, Hardcover.
ISBN 3-86187-075-4
26,80 DM

Bruno Gmünder Verlag
Postfach 11 07 29
10837 Berlin

EDITION EUROS

■ BRUNO GMÜNDER